CRIMINAL JUSTICE SYSTEM

My Experience and the Way Forward

CRIMINAL JUSTICE SYSTEM

My Experience and the Way Forward

Davinder Pal Singh

Vivekananda International Foundation

PENTAGON PRESS LLP

First published in 2023 by

PENTAGON PRESS LLP
206, Peacock Lane, Shahpur Jat
New Delhi-110049, India
Contact: 011-64706243

Typeset in Adobe Garamond, 11.5 Point
Printed by Aegean Offset Printers, Greater Noida, U.P.

ISBN 978-93-90095-84-1 (HB)

www.pentagonpress.in

CONTENTS

FOREWORD

The Vivekananda International Foundation is happy to publish the book *Criminal Justice System: My Experience and the Way Forward* by Davinder Pal Singh, Visiting Fellow, VIF. He is an Advocate with an experience of 33 years of practice in criminal cases in various Indian courts including the Supreme Court.

It is widely recognized that India's more than century-old criminal justice system is outdated and is in need of urgent reforms. As India rises politically, economically & socially, it must reform its governance system and the rule of law. Judicial reforms are a part of India's renewal in the 21st century. In 2000, the Ministry of Home Affairs had set up a committee on the reform of the judicial system under Justice V.S. Malimath, former Chief Justice of the Karnataka and Kerala High Courts. The Committee submitted its report in 2003. Looking into the various aspects of the criminal justice system, the committee made 158 recommendations which, unfortunately, have yet to be implemented. The Law Commission of India is also studying the question amendment to the Indian Penal Code, 1860, Code of Criminal Procedure, 1973, and the Indian Evidence Act, 1872.

In the meanwhile, the pendency of cases in the courts has increased manifold, the jails are overcrowded with under-trial prisoners. Trials are stretched to decades, making the task of getting justice from the courts expensive and stressful. To make matters worse, the judicial system is finding it difficult to keep pace with the task of dealing with the new age crimes.

Drawing from his vast experience, Sh DP Singh pinpoints what is wrong with the Indian criminal justice system and how it can be improved.

He looks at the various stages of criminal justice examining it from the point of view of multiple stakeholders including the victim, accused and their families, society, investigators, judges, public prosecutors, jails, and media. He dispassionately analyses the key aspects of criminal justice including investigation, pre-trial proceedings, trials, and post-trial stages. Various chapters of the book look closely into specific issues such as arrest, bail, cross-examination, sentencing, etc. The author familiarising the reader to the practical realities of the system and propose solutions. This concise but lucidly written book avoids excessive legal jargon and is accessible to the lay reader.

The broad conclusion of the book is that while India's global stature is growing, the rule-of-law in the area of criminal justice is reducing. The common man needs to have quick and affordable access to criminal justice. Investigations must be impartial. Trials must be done and concluded expeditiously. The autonomy of the lower judiciary must be protected. The author notes that judges often do not have the necessary experience in conducting trials in criminal cases. The situation must change. Finally, investigators, lawyers and judges must have high moral and ethical standards. Otherwise, the faith of the citizen in justice system would be eroded.

The book raises pertinent questions regarding the state of health of criminal justice in India. It also offers practical solutions. I am confident that the book will encourage a debate on the subject.

New Delhi
05 Dec 2022

Dr Arvind Gupta
Director
The Vivekananda International Foundation

ACKNOWLEDGEMENTS

I would like to express my heartfelt gratitude to all those who have contributed to the creation of this book and my journey as a humble student of law.

To my clients, who shared their stories with me and gave me an insight into the realities that lie beyond the legal jargon that typically follows such incidents. It has been a privilege to represent you and fight for your rights.

To the judges who have presided over these cases, thank you for your wisdom and quest to decide the cases. Your decisions have helped shape the legal landscape, which continues to expand through scrutiny by the higher courts. Even the errors made by you contributed to the evolution of legal principles, although many areas/legal questions still need to be ironed out.

To my seniors, who taught me how to interpret laws and understand the intricacies of law during trial and appeal. I will always remember and treasure the valuable lessons I learned during my early days from Sh. Dinesh Mathur, Senior Advocate, and the finer nuances of the profession that I gained from Mr. R.S. Cheema, Senior Advocate. Mr. Cheema, my *Guru*, is responsible for simulating and provoking my thought process and igniting my passions beyond the field of law.

I would like to extend my appreciation to my family, who never complained about the long hours I had to put into my profession, which often came at their expense.

I also thank Hon'ble Mr. Justice Vibhu Bakhru of the Delhi High Court and Dr. K.P. Singh, Former DGP, Haryana, both of whom gave their valuable inputs and time during the preliminary discussions on the book at VIF.

Advocates Manu Mishra and Shreya Dutt were instrumental in making this book a reality, thanks to their tireless discussions, extensive dictation sessions, and countless revisions to the script.

I am grateful to VIF for pushing me to write this book, particularly Dr. Arvind Gupta, Ambassador Satish Chandra, and Lt. General R.K. Sawhney. I am also grateful to all those who have supported and inspired me along the way, including my peers and colleagues.

I would like to conclude by expressing my gratitude to the publisher Pentagon Press LLP for the unyielding support in the process.

D.P. Singh

CRIMINAL JUSTICE SYSTEM

I STAKE HOLDERS

1. Victim & Family
2. Accused & Family
3. Society
4. Investigator
5. Judges (Courts)
6. Public Prosecutors
7. Lawyers
8. Jails
9. Press & Media

II INVESTIGATION

1. Role of:
   - a. Police
   - b. Witnesses
   - c. Accused
   - d. Other suspects (not witnesses)
2. Registration of a Case
3. Arrest, Custody, Bail & Remand
4. Search & Seizure
5. Attachment & Confiscation
6. Forensic & Medical Investigation

III PRE-TRIAL PROCEEDINGS

1. Notice under S.91 CrPC
2. Chargesheet
3. Cognizance
4. Stage of compliance under S.207 CrPC (Supply of Documents)
5. Committal of Cases
6. Letters of Request

IV TRIAL

1. Trial Strategy
2. Charge
3. Evidence
4. Art of Cross-Examination
5. Summoning of Additional Accused
6. Arguments
7. Judgment
8. Consequences & Considerations of Sentencing

V POST TRIAL

1. Appeal
2. Bail in Appeal
3. Additional Evidence & other proceedings
4. Parole
5. Remission
6. Pardon

LIST OF ABBREVIATIONS

CBI	Central Bureau of Investigation
CCTV	Closed Circuit Television
CrPC	Code of Criminal Procedure
DDR	Daily Diary Register
DDT	Deception Detection Test
FIR	First Information Report
FSL	Forensic Science Laboratory
IO	Investigating Officer
IPC	Indian Penal Code
Ld.	Learned
LRs	Letters of Request/Letters Rogatory
MHA	Ministry of Home Affairs
MLAT	Mutual Legal Assistance Treaty
MoU	Memorandum of Understanding
NDPS	Narcotic Drugs and Psychotropic Substances
NIA	National Investigation Agency
P.S.	Police Station
PMLA	Prevention of Money Laundering Act
PP	Public Prosecutor
RERA	Real Estate Regulatory Authority
S.	Section

SC	Supreme Court
SEBI	Securities and Exchange Board of India
SHO	Station House Officer
u/s	Under Section
UAPA	Unlawful Activities Prevention Act
USA	United States of America

INTRODUCTION

'Criminal Justice System: My Experience and the Way Forward' is in essence my experience of more than 30 years in the study and practice of criminal trials in India. This book is a practical guide of my experience. I have represented both the private clients in their capacity as accused or victims and have represented the Government as a Special Prosecutor or the Additional Advocate General. Through this journey, I have seen all aspects of a criminal trial across a variety of cases, including violent crimes, crimes against women, economic offences. My experiences range from district courts and High Courts across states, going right up to the Supreme Court. This experience has facilitated my exposure to various facets of the Criminal Justice System. This book is as such my perspective of the Criminal Justice System, and I do not claim to be correct in all my opinions or perceptions.

What prompted me to pen down my views was my dissatisfaction with the current functioning of the system and the desire to address and overcome its limitations. I aim to dissect the obvious and underlying problems in the system and propose practical solutions. My intention is not to criticize but only encourage the implementation of the law already in place in its true spirit. While emphasising on the need for the system to adapt and evolve with changes in law, society, trends and beliefs, I aim to introduce the readers to the practical realities of the system.

This book is likely to resonate with one and all, who have at any point of time interacted with any aspect of the Criminal Justice System, or are likely to have a brush with the Criminal Justice System. While some might find the writing style to be too simplistic, this is a deliberate attempt to make the common man understand how the system works. Therefore, the legal jargon has been kept to the bare minimum.

My attempt in this book is to give the reader a step-by-step insight into the system. For the same reason, the First Chapter introduces the 9 stakeholders of the Criminal Justice System. Whenever a crime is committed, each stakeholder and, or their family, is directly or indirectly affected by the crime, and participates in the journey of the crime. The book as such starts with an insight as to who are these stakeholders, how are they or their families affected by crime, the impact they have on other stakeholders and the system as a whole. The reader can pick up this book, place himself in the shoes of the stakeholder (or not and read it as a whole), and understand the workings of Criminal Justice System—what is the procedure and its purpose, what to expect from the system, what they can or cannot do vis-à-vis their rights and restrictions in law. The book also deals with the harsh realities surrounding each such stakeholder and recommends remedial steps.

Further, the book delves into the journey of a crime, right from the offence being committed till the final adjudication of the case. As such, the book is divided into Chapters including investigation, inquiry, trial and post-trial proceedings. In each chapter, an endeavour has been made to account for the main steps involved, while also bringing to fore the changes in implementation or enactment of law required.

The book is as such not an encyclopaedia of the system. It is more of a guide which takes you through the important aspects and stages involved in the system; also justifying the rationale behind the need to change the existing law. The book suggests both structural and systemic reforms that are consistent with the constitutional ethos. Emphasis is as such laid on expeditious investigation and trial, while also recommending the creation of an effective redressal mechanism which facilitates easy access to all stakeholders. The book advocates the reformation and rehabilitation of offenders, also suggesting other measures aimed at balancing the rights and interests of the victim, the accused and the society at large.

The book by and large emphasises on the need to adopt a futuristic approach rather than a reactive one, while understanding the manner in which the Criminal Justice System operates. I implore all readers to have a vision in mind, use logic and creativity to device solutions, and further not be solely driven by technicalities to improve our existing system.

I

STAKEHOLDERS

1. INTRODUCTION

There are nine important stakeholders in the Criminal Justice System: the victims and their families; accused and their families; society; investigator; judges (through courts); public prosecutors; lawyers, jails; and the press and media. Each stakeholder at some point of time is either a catalyst of justice or directly affected by the outcome of the criminal justice system. Even though these stakeholders hold strong and independent positions, they have co-existed in the criminal justice system since centuries. This chapter seeks to explain the role and importance of each stakeholder and the impact of their interaction with the other stakeholders. At the outset, it is crucial to understand the symbiotic relationship that exists between the stakeholders in order to garner a true and practical insight into the working of the system. The first step towards this is to study: (1) role of different stakeholders; (2) their rights, (3) their interests; (4) their entitlements; (5) impact on other stakeholders, and then to assess how the impact ties in with the larger working of our criminal justice system. Over the years, a myopic view of each stakeholder and the impact and participation in the system has been adopted. In this chapter, an attempt has been made to delve deeper into their roles, both individually and collectively.

This chapter is factual and is a matter of fact. However, the discussion is important and needs to be explained at the very beginning of the book to put it into its correct perspective. It should be read as it is and the detailing, wherever required, has been dealt with in subsequent chapters.

2. Victims and their Families

Role

The role of a victim in the Indian criminal justice system is mostly of a mere witness and otherwise of a mere spectator in a trial. Apart from giving initial information to the police and recording his testimony in court, the victim generally does not play an active role in the case. This is because the state assumes the responsibility of protecting the interests of the victim and society, also taking control of the investigation and trial. The guiding concern is to try the offenders for the commission of the offence and, resultantly, provide retribution to the victim.

Interest

Due to the diverse nature of Indian society, the victims' accessibility to the criminal justice system and their rights are often contingent on and determined by their social and economic standing. For instance, victims belonging to the economically weaker sections of society or minority social groups usually have a difficult time in approaching the police or engaging a lawyer. In such cases, if the offenders belong to powerful families, they may influence the system to their unfair advantage at the cost of the victim. Similarly, if the victims possess considerable social and economic capital, they may misuse their status to initiate malicious and motivated prosecutions. Either way, aside from the law, the interest of the victims has a lot to do with their status in society.

Rights and Entitlements

Victims possess certain rights granted to them under law. They are entitled to lodge an FIR in the police station, and this need not be in the form of a written complaint. They also have the right to assist the PP during the trial. Further, the victims have also been granted a statutory right to appeal against any acquittal or inadequate sentence imposed on the accused. Though rarely invoked, victims and their dependants have the right to get adequate compensation when they have suffered loss or injury arising from the offence and/or are consequently in need of rehabilitation.

The apex court, very recently in the *Lakhimpur Kheri* case, held that the victims have a right to be heard and participate at every stage of the investigation and trial. The import and implications of the observation will be seen and felt over a period of time.

Harsh Realities and Impact

The victims' lack of awareness and education about their rights makes them vulnerable to arbitrary treatment by the police. For example, it is common practice for either the police to write the complaint on behalf of the victim to suit a particular narrative or turn the victim away to first get a written complaint for them to register a case. Such a practice results in deviating from and diluting the facts. Often, the victim is clueless about what he or she has submitted in the complaint. Often, the complaint is written solely from the perspective of the policeman or lawyer with the objective of making a case worthy of proof in court by exaggerating the allegations, or to get a suitable settlement.

Victims from marginalized sections are often coerced by the police to change their testimonies and statements to suit the fabricated versions of the prosecution. Also, in certain high-profile cases, the victim is sometimes used as a pawn by the police in furthering their own agenda against the accused or garnering publicity for the case. Under such circumstances, it is critical to protect the victims and their families. There is a dire need for implementing a statutory scheme specifically designed for the protection of victims in India. While there exists a witness protection scheme, there is no legislative enactment to specifically offer protection to victims. Such a scheme can encourage victims to come forward and file their complaints without fear of life or harassment.

On the other hand, so-called victims, who are powerful, influential, vigilant and/or are aware of their legal rights, tend to misuse the judicial process to take revenge or blackmail the accused. In this scenario, it is the victim who holds power and abuses the legal machinery to fulfil his vendetta or suit his gains. This is also seen in cases where the victim plans to extort money from the accused based on a false complaint. Examples of these can be seen in cases of cruelty and dowry harassment where victims file frivolous litigations to harass the accused and their family.

A victim, in ideal terms, is someone who has suffered injury or loss and approaches the criminal justice system to seek justice. During the judicial process, his life changes drastically due to such process coupled with the injury and loss sustained. The sense of injustice and being wrongly treated brings a lot of discontent and makes the victim an anti-establishment force or, in certain cases, a nuisance, who may choose to take the law into his own hands. Counselling, rehabilitative methods, and medical and monetary aid are key factors which can help in easing the internal turmoil brewing within the victim and his family.

A balance needs to be maintained to enhance and improve the issues of the victim's accessibility to the criminal justice system and ensure that economically or socially vulnerable victims are not exploited. It is also prudent to be circumspect and keep the victim's role limited. The investigation and trial must not be swayed by the victim's emotions and possible exaggerations.

3. Accused and the Families

Role and Interest

An accused is the most important stakeholder in the criminal justice system and is directly affected by the effectiveness and quality of the system. An accused is alleged to have acted in derogation of the law and order of society and shaken the peace and security of the system. He could be anyone from our society; from rich to poor, illiterate to holding the highest degree of education, a man of good reputation or a man who has been living the life of a criminal.

The perception of an accused varies from case to case and there are various shades of an accused. While the accused could be the actual culprit, it is equally possible that he himself is a victim, that is, entangled in false or malicious complaints which are an outcome of revenge or rivalries. We must remember and appreciate that an accused is not a convicted criminal and must be treated fairly and impartially safeguarded. Other stakeholders of the system must strictly ensure that an accused is not branded as a 'villain' and does not suffer for alleged offences, none of which have yet been proven to be committed by him.

An accused is at the centre stage of the criminal justice system. A fair trial is integral to ensure that the faith of the accused in the criminal justice system remains intact. If the truth is uncovered after investigation, the accused who is guilty may accept his fate. However, to the contrary, if the investigation or trial is plagued with arbitrariness, then the confidence of the accused to misuse the system may be further strengthened.

Rights and Entitlement

An accused has a presumption of innocence in his favour, until he is proven guilty. He has been given certain rights under law to ensure a fair chance to put forward his defence. Such rights include receiving all information concerning his case, protection from being coerced or threatened by the police, refraining from making statements that may incriminate him, to be represented by a lawyer of his choice or have access to legal aid, even during police custody.

Fairness in dealing with an accused also entails that his liberty, though subject to reasonable restrictions, should not be excessively and mindlessly curtailed. In fact, every accused is entitled to bail as a rule and his freedom must be restricted only under exceptional circumstances, recognized by law, which is the triple test, that is, if the person is likely to abscond, tamper with evidence, or influence witnesses.

We must appreciate that an accused does not belong behind bars for mere allegations of committing an offence. Even the restrictions placed on the liberty of the accused such as judicial custody, attachment and seizure of property, and travel restrictions have a negative impact on his and his family's life, reputation and livelihood. Thus, these decisions must be taken after careful thought and consideration of the facts and circumstances of the case.

The freedom and liberty of the accused should be curtailed in some serious cases which impact society at large so as shock society's conscience or, in cases which have a grave economic impact on a large number of people. For example, the *Nirbhaya* case or cases of ponzi schemes which take away or *loot* poor or marginalized people.

It should shock the societal and judicial conscience when such liberties are curtailed as a norm and not as an exception. The onus on the courts is even more when the accused before it is from the marginalized sections of society or is accused of petty or not so serious offences. It is shocking that many people have been in jail for years due to their inability to furnish a bail bond or for the unawareness of their own rights or for the lack of proper representation before courts.

Impact

Upon the initiation of a case, there is a lot of pressure on the accused. There is equal, if not more, pressure on his family, which also suffers from social stigma, harassment, depleting financial resources, loss of livelihood and the like. This leads to great misery for the accused and his family. Such is the environment today that the moment someone is declared an accused, he and his family are stigmatized without any decision on his guilt. The family is often left to fend for itself while being burdened with the litigation expenses of the accused. They also find it difficult to get respectable jobs and are often forced to resort to a life of crime to make money for a living.

Way Forward

Today, the expression 'justice must be seen to be done' is often misused by investigators. Arbitrary arrests to show progress in investigation results in continued incarceration of accused pending trial. This not only cuts off the societal ties of the accused but also affects his ability to prepare his defence. Guilty or not guilty, the system must endeavour to ensure that the life of an accused or his family does not crumble. Mere accusations without a conclusive decision must not stigmatize the accused and his family.

An endeavour must be made to reduce the number of undertrial prisoners in jail unless they fail to meet the triple test. Even in situations where bail is denied, jails must facilitate a proper setup for lawyer-and-family meetings of the accused. Except large metropolitan cities, the system throughout the country needs an overhaul.

There is also differential treatment accorded to accused. A poor man perishes while the rich and powerful exert their influence and manipulate the process. The system must ensure that an individual does not succumb to the whims and fancies of the influential. While implementing the law, it must not be forgotten that the end goal of the system is not respite or revenge but rehabilitation, restoration, and order in society. Pushing the accused into jail is counterproductive as it enables alleged first-time offenders to learn tips and tricks from other hardened criminals, and these interactions further encourage them to commit more crimes. While there are jail manuals and rules to treat undertrials differently from convicts, the implementation requires improvement. Often, the accused realise that jails, which provide a range of amenities such as food, medicine, and the like, are far more luxurious than their lives outside. Rather than earning honest money, they prefer to stay in jail or keep committing petty offences to re-enter jails.

Thus, the criminal justice system must recognise the socio-economic realities of society while dealing with the accused. The law must work in conjunction with the ground reality, failing which, the quote of Sir Benjamin Franklin impressing upon hundred guilty persons going unpunished as being better than one innocent person suffering shall stand out only as a cruel irony.

4. Society

Role and Interest

Society is an important stakeholder in the criminal justice system. The representation of the State on behalf of the complainant is primarily because crime is against society at large. Accordingly, the State conducts prosecutions on behalf of complainants.

Society is the place that one lives in. The behaviour of a group of people is influenced by society, that is, the people around them. Without going into the sociological or anthropological paradigm of society, it is sufficient to mention that society is referred to as the general behaviour of the people living in that environment, their ethos, their economic standing, their social and educational awareness, their culture, their religion, and the like. Depending on society, the two factors which take the centre stage are caste and economic standing. This becomes more pronounced depending on whether society is rural or urban.

Society's image of the criminal justice system comes from the neighbourhood or community. Such perceptions are made from the dominant view of the concerned society. This view is an amalgamation of the vested interests of individuals and their standing in society, ideologies based on religion, caste or creed, media, personal experiences and/or personal ties with the victim or accused or their families. All such considerations are passed from person to person. This eventually shapes public perception of the system, more specifically about 'crime' and 'criminals' through various modes including debates, rallies, protests, and the like.

In fact, all stakeholders are a product of society and the nature and extent of crime is often a reflection of the society's own perception and response to it. Thus, as society progresses, crime also evolves and becomes more nuanced. The rise in a particular type of crime is often contingent upon or a result of the social and political environment prevalent in society. For instance, the increasing focus on women's issues and their legal and social vulnerabilities in public discourse, while a liberating change, has resulted in the rise of false registration of cases of harassment, rape, and dowry. Similarly, with technological advancement, there has been a rise in complaints of cyber-crimes, internet fraud and even white-collar crimes.

Rights and Entitlements

Earlier, India had a jury system which ensured greater societal participation in trials. This was however done away with since Indian society and jurors were found to be prone to manipulation and influenced by extraneous factors. As a result, the outcome of a case was often contingent on the jury's prejudices and biases, rather than law.

Nevertheless, countries such as the USA, Canada, and Australia, among others, still successfully continue to conduct jury trials after carefully screening jurors for their prejudices and propensities. In fact, in the USA, the 'Right to a Jury Trial' is a constitutional right.

The situation is quite the opposite in India where, except for reporting cases or being witnesses, society has no active role in the system and is a mere onlooker. The law mandates that no third party has any right in a criminal trial.

Impact

Society has a direct nexus with the evolution of law. Laws are implemented not only for acting as a deterrent against the erring individuals but also to instil 'public confidence' in the system. In recent years, changes have been brought in law to address public discontent and garner support. This was seen in the *Nirbhaya* case, where the outrage and reaction of society to the heinous offences led to amendments to the Indian Penal Code and the Juvenile Justice Act. Though this was the need of the hour, we must not forget that this was also a result of the reaction of society and the surrounding politics. Another such instance can be seen in terms of the *Jan Lokpal* movement headed by Anna Hazare which paved the way for the Lokpal and Lokayukta Act, 2013.

Investigators and judges, who are also a part of society, often find themselves at the crossroads and are susceptible to 'popular' societal notions rather than objective views. Further, since a crime is a crime against society, the final decision of the case has a bearing on society. Anyone can identify themselves with either the victim or the falsely named accused or a motivated victim. The outcome of the case determines the satisfaction of society and their general content or discontent with the system.

Need of the Hour

While it is necessary to enhance and increase society's participation in the administration of justice, it is equally necessary to maintain objectivity and keep society at an arm's length from policies, statutory changes and more specifically investigations. While looking for changes to be brought into the system, often governed by societal sentiments, we must not forget the alternative paths that are forgotten and can be the best way forward.

Today, there is a need to sensitize society towards the rights of the victims and the accused, as well as the duties and role of different stakeholders in the criminal justice system to ensure their effective contribution. This can be done through public education beginning with a basic course curriculum in schools and colleges, or through awareness and educational programmes, and by improving transparency and accountability in the system. Public dissemination of information, which gives an actual insight into the functioning of the system, will help enhance society's ability to critically evaluate the content that they consume and help increase their objectivity.

5. Investigator

Role and Interest

In common parlance, an investigator is identified as the Investigating Officer ('IO'). His primary role is to conduct a speedy, effective and fair investigation. While a random officer and most likely a *munshi* at the police station is the first point of contact for a complainant to report the commission of an offence, post registration of an FIR, it is the investigator who becomes the point of contact for society to report and receive information about any incident. The investigator sets the ball rolling with the kind of investigation he undertakes. He plays an important role in ensuring justice for one and all, including the victims or the accused.

An investigator is generally between the rank of an Assistant Sub-Inspector and Deputy Superintendent of Police, depending on the nature and seriousness of the case. He is entrusted with finding the truth. In his pursuit of truth, he must search, collect and analyse evidence regardless of whether it favours the victim or the accused. He must present a *bona fide* report of his opinion to the court. His aim is not to ensure that the strongest case to secure a conviction is made out. His duty is not to further determine the guilt of the accused. His duty is simply to facilitate the court in arriving at a final decision. Under law, he is free to formulate an opinion to close the investigation if he feels that no case is made out.

Rights and Entitlements

Investigation is the sole domain of the investigator. He is the one entrusted with the mode and manner of conducting it and is driven by his discretion and expertise. Even the courts can only seek his opinion on an aspect of the investigation but cannot interfere with his opinion. It is essential that investigators discharge their duties in an impartial and fair manner.

Impact

A fair and qualified investigator will help victims get justice. At the same time, he will also ensure that no individual is harassed or treated unfairly, and that the rights of the accused and his family are secure. His dealings with the victims and the accused as well as their respective families go a long way in determining the perception of the public towards the police. His final report is in fact the foundation stone for any court to arrive at a decision and determine the guilt or innocence of the accused.

Need of the Hour

While the problems in the system have been dealt with at appropriate places in this book, some broad observations need to be mentioned at the outset. These will go a long way in understanding the realities of the system and proposed solutions.

Investigators, who generally belong to the rank of an Inspector/Sub-inspector, do not have any separate qualifying examinations and the entry-level exams to the force do not specifically assess their competency as an investigator. To this effect, it is crucial that an investigator receives the requisite training to become skilled and efficient. They must also be trained to use scientific methods that aid in an effective investigation. For example, very few crimes today can be solved by traditional policing. The Supreme Court realised the importance of scientific investigation in the 1990s itself. With the advancement in technology, the understanding of scientific investigation tools is the way forward to solve most crimes. The requisite skill, competence and training to use the same are key to a good investigation. There is however no strait-jacket formula to investigate a particular crime. The investigator should use his discretion to adopt the traditional way of investigation or avail any of the scientific tools necessary for a fair and effective investigation.

While dealing with the victims and the accused or their representatives, the investigator must be sensitised and made aware of his role and responsibilities.

There is also a need for a systematic change in the structure of the police setup, which is entrusted with both law and order duties as well as investigation responsibilities. Many a time, police officers and investigators are directed to carry out *bandobasth* duties such as VIP movement vigilance, patrolling, and the like. While getting involved in law and order as well as investigation duties, the investigator is sometimes forced to compromise on the quality of investigation. There is thus, a dire need to effectively segregate the investigation wing of the police from law and order responsibilities. This will help ensure that investigators get the best environment and maximum time to carry out their duties.

Investigators must also learn to exercise power judiciously. They possess unfettered authority to carry out investigation and are responsible for exercising it within the strict ambit of the law. While practical experiences justify vesting such power with them, it should not be left unchecked for the investigator to abuse and achieve concocted or biased results. Examples of such misuse of powers are deviations in protocol, harassment of victims or accused, custodial torture, unnecessary arrests, coercion and duress. The training programme must teach investigators the need to exercise restraint and due caution, as it not only results in conservation of time, manpower and resources but also upholds the credibility of the criminal justice system by improving public perception.

Investigators are also sometimes responsible for padding of cases, that is, exaggerating facts or concealing vital information in a case as they are either influenced or pressurised by rich and powerful victims, accused or their own seniors. The law already envisages this possibility of abuse of powers. There is a dire need to give these provisions teeth and initiate a practice of accountability. A simple solution would be for the courts to hold the investigators strictly accountable for any such violation by defining parameters and not overlook these deviations under the umbrella of 'in furtherance of investigation'. This will ensure that investigators do not work under pressure of achieving maximum convictions and promotions, but instead focus on finding out the truth.

6. Judges (Through Courts)

Role and Interest

The court is the caretaker and guardian of the stakeholders in the criminal justice system. It is an important institution manned by a judge. As an institution, it safeguards the rights of each individual and stakeholder, acting as a redressal mechanism to instil public faith and confidence in the efficacy of the system. Courts also shape the law of the land and how it must be interpreted and exercised. A judge, vested with the powers of the court, assumes such power and responsibility and plays a vital role in the administration and dispensation of justice. An ideal judge can transform lives while an ideal judiciary can transform the nation by instilling the Rule of Law.

Rights and Entitlements

Under law, the judge exercises a general supervision and control over all facets of a criminal case, that is, investigation, inquiry or trial. At the first stage, the judge has the power to sieve false allegations to ensure a proper utilisation of the resources and machinery. During the investigation and inquiry, the judge must oversee the protection of the rights of the victim, the accused and the investigator. He has ample powers to ensure the safety and well-being of the victims and the accused, their families, and also to ensure fair treatment is meted out to them. He also has powers to aid in the investigation. During the trial, he has ample powers to get evidence tendered to find out the truth. However, throughout, a judge is barred from applying his own theories, adding or subtracting evidence, or putting forth his own beliefs and values, although there are times when we see a departure from the rule. A judge also has an inherent protection to his actions in good faith. His decision cannot be called into question. He is only under the supervisory control of a higher court.

Impact

By the very nature of his role, the type of justice that a judge delivers impacts society. Society looks up to the courts. The courts, through judges, instil that confidence in the citizens of the general sense of justice through their words. Such is the impact of the judges that even citizens who have doubts on the judge or the court still look upon it for redressal when the other stakeholders of the system fail them.

Need of the Hour

The judge should ensure that the checks and balances in the system are not disturbed. He must actively look into issues of false prosecutions, exaggerated complaints, abuse of rights and powers, delayed trials and also take steps to deter all parties from resorting to such tactics.

The practice of courts in giving certain concessions to the police should not over-extend to one of condoning laxity. This should be strictly followed to keep the police on its toes and prompt them to conduct investigation in a fair and transparent manner. In fact, the judge should deal with false or malicious cases and the inadequate or negligent discharge of duties by the investigator in the same proceedings to save time and ensure accountability.

The personal preferences of the judge should not overshadow his decisions. He must keep aside his own ideologies or those of society that he is associated with. He must not let the opinion of the media or public sentiments or even his own perceptions influence him in deciding a case. Political preferences and personal equations must be kept aside for fair adjudication of cases. While a judge is the voice of society, he does not represent it and must not be swayed by its opinion. He is only to be swayed by the statute and rule of law, while solely considering the evidence brought before him. At the same time, he must also strive to not let mere technicalities lead to victimisation and should take active steps to prevent the abuse of the process of law. In fact, it should be the endeavour of a judge to promote easier access to justice. The judge is often called upon to resolve this conflict between law and society. This has resulted in the evolution of law, keeping in mind changing society and practical realities.

A judge, as the custodian of all stakeholders, has the prime responsibility of ensuring that justice is done. He must discharge his powers in a way that no individual is harassed or treated unfairly. Both the accused and the victim are aware of the true nature of the events and as such, any fair decision will only enhance their faith in the system. As a way forward a Judge's powers should not and must not remain unchecked and he must be held accountable for his failure to discharge his duties. A mechanism should be devised by Supreme Court as a self-regulation measure.

This book, in the subsequent chapters, deals with the role of courts and their powers, while also identifying solutions to help them overcome their limitations.

7. Public Prosecutor (PP)

Role and Interest

The PP is an indispensable stakeholder in any criminal justice system. The PP assists the courts in upholding the rule of law. In India, the office of the PP is of a public servant holding a statutory office. The expectation from the PP is not to merely to secure a conviction, but rather to ensure that justice is meted out to the victim or the accused, as the case may be. His responsibility makes his role more difficult, since he is to not only attempt and secure convictions, but also to see that an innocent man does not suffer. Designed to be an independent office comprising of the good law officers, the office of the PP in India presently faces a credibility crisis, which has been briefly described in this chapter.

Rights and Entitlements

The PP, as an officer of the court, is not strictly bound by the instructions of the state machinery, more specifically during a trial. While his role during the stage of investigation is limited and he can only assist in curing the loopholes of investigation in a charge sheet, it is post investigation that his role becomes paramount.

It is his discretion in theory whether he wants an accused to turn approver or whether he wants to withdraw the prosecution against an accused. He is further empowered to not press charges against an accused, should he feel that there are not enough grounds of proceeding against the accused.

Impact

The trial is conducted by the PP and, in his absence, the trial will come to a standstill. The PP can make any witness an approver, he can drop any witness, choose to examine a witness not cited by police or withdraw the prosecution completely should no case be made out, in his opinion.

Need of the Hour

A fair PP will ensure that the victim or the accused get justice, depending upon the facts and circumstances of the case.

However, as things stand today, the office of the PP is marred with an array of problems requiring immediate redressal. When the new CrPC came into force in 1973, one of the most important changes attempted to be achieved was to separate the prosecution wing from the police, since the PPs till then were a part of the police. While the PPs have since been placed under the Directorate of Prosecution, it has been felt time and again that they act hand in glove with the investigating agency or follow executive orders.

This issue can be addressed by simply fixing and devising a transparent system for appointment of PPs. Though the process is clearly defined, all states in India do not uniformly adhere to it, with some devising their own processes. In fact, several states have ousted the requirement to consult with courts and exercise unbridled power in the appointment process. The widespread concern in civil society about this resulted in a reference being sent by the Prime Minister's Office to the Law Commission, highlighting the issue of state governments amending the law and unilaterally appointing PPs.

PPs also need to be given proper training and remuneration. This would encourage better legal minds to opt for the office of the PP. Proper training and infrastructure will help increase competence associated with the office of the PP. Accordingly, the office of the PP must be sanctioned appropriate infrastructure for research, filings, personnel support and such other provisions for the preparation of cases.

The lack of infrastructural support is evident throughout since the PPs do not even have the tools to store and carry files for preparation. Despite the large volume of cases, they end up reading the files in court the very day of the trial and primarily rely on the police for the briefing, with little or no application of mind. As such, the PP, more so in small cities, is not even recognisable in court despite having the same rank, in essence, as a judge in the administration of justice. To address these concerns, PPs should be provided with a virtual library and computers to facilitate easy and simple access to case files and documents, more so with e-filings and virtual hearings becoming the norm. PPs should also be assisted by a competent team so that the workload is carefully distributed and allocated.

8. LAWYERS

Role and Interest

Lawyers are entrusted with the responsibility of representing their clients so as to achieve the best possible result for them. At the same time, a lawyer, as an officer, must also perform his duty of assisting the courts to discharge quality and timely justice. This is often ignored and invariably the system suffers.

Lawyers represent the victim, complainant or an accused. Apart from these, the lawyers may also represent any third party in a case affecting their rights. A lawyer may also be directed to provide a neutral opinion on the case for assisting the court and helping it navigate through any complex questions of law or dichotomies. On such occasions, the lawyer wears the cap of *amicus curiae* (friend of the court). There are also lawyers who do not represent any individual but a large group of similarly placed individuals for furthering a social cause.

Rights and Entitlements

A lawyer appearing in court is entitled to a right of audience for his client in the court. He is further entitled to make filings for his client. In addition, a lawyer is entitled to act as per the authority given to him by his client, including interacting with law enforcement agencies and accepting and sending documents on behalf of the client. In lieu of all such functions performed by the lawyer, he is entitled to such professional fees as may be agreed upon with his client. However, such fees cannot be contingent or cannot form a share of a favourable final judgment for his client.

Impact

Often, the tenacity and advocacy skills of a lawyer prompt the courts to dig deeper into issues and unravel solutions. History has shown that lawyers who can offer quality assistance have shaped laws and policies having a great impact on society. Such quality assistance more importantly helps in reducing the pendency of cases.

The ethical discharge of duties by lawyers includes the duty to keep the best interests of clients in the forefront. However, bending the rules or going beyond the duties prescribed for lawyers in the Advocates Act or Bar Council Rules for a favourable result, is unbecoming of a lawyer. Taking repeated adjournments as a strategy to delay the process of law, appearing before court whilst unprepared, over-charging and under-performing are acts classified as unscrupulous and deter the faith and confidence in lawyers as well as the legal fraternity. Frivolous or motivated litigations are often initiated upon legal advice. Approaching multiple or incorrect forums for relief leading to wastage of time and resources of both the courts and the parties are also spearheaded by lawyers.

Need of the Hour

The Bar Council of India has framed rules which enumerate and differentiate between an advocate's duty towards the court, his clients, his opponents as well as other fellow advocates. A lawyer thus, has different shades and duties, all of which he or she must simultaneously uphold and maintain. Ethical and virtuous performance of lawyers must be encouraged especially amongst the large number of young lawyers entering this profession each year. Though years of practice makes one wise, the foundation for becoming a principled lawyer is formed in the nascent years of the profession.

Since access to justice is the need of the hour, lawyers are encouraged to provide legal aid and take up cases where they are not driven by monetary considerations but public service. Legal aid seeks to serve those members of society who are helpless and would be subjected to endless suffering if they are not steered through the legal processes. This is where lawyers step in and play a very important role in the upliftment of society and ensuring smoother facilitation of justice.

9. JAILS

Role and Interest

A jail, being a correctional facility, is viewed as a symbol of justice by the public. It is essentially a place for rehabilitating and reforming prisoners and ensure that public order is restored.

Although traditionally, and as a general belief, jails are correction centres, are they? If one closely studies the journey of the jail manual and rules in the past years, or for that matter the prevalent culture in jails, the results are far from satisfactory.

More undertrials perishing in jail

Earlier, jails used to consist of more convicted prisoners than undertrials. This situation however stands reversed today. The number of undertrials perishing in jails is alarming. Earlier, the practice of keeping convicted prisoners separately was carefully followed but today, this practice has been diluted which has resulted in the intermixing of hardened convicts and undertrials. This is a huge risk as far as the psyche of the undertrial inmates is concerned. While in earlier times, the undertrials were mostly accused of violent crimes, this situation has changed with the evolution of society. This is evident from the fact that somewhere in the post 1980s, after changes in law fixated on women empowerment, the number of sexual offenders in jails increased. At present, offenders of white-collar crimes are overcrowding jails.

Conditions and environment of jails

Internationally, a common ground for resisting extradition proceedings is the inhumane conditions of jails in India. While the state is now coming up with model jails, the situation is far from convincing. If we inspect the overall condition of jails across the country, at least 90 per cent of the jails will fall short of meeting the threshold of even the most basic humane conditions.

Courts have time and again cautioned jail authorities against jails being a hub of illegal activities rather than a deterrent of crime. Such an environment adversely affects the inmates who, having lost societal ties and having nothing to lose, get further involved in crimes.

Another issue looming over the distressing situation in jails is overcrowding. While this is a serious issue which has been pointed out time and again by the courts, in juxtaposition, bail jurisprudence practised in India is also a culprit. The courts, except a few landmark judgments, have been reluctant in granting bail, which has resulted in overcrowding of jails.

Need of the Hour and Changing Trends in Jails

By its very nature, a jail is a different world. The importance given to the jailor with regard to his responsibility for changing and correcting people has disintegrated over time. Today, jailors are often responsible for the crime syndicate in jails. One can gauge the changing trends in jails through movies. The iconic feature film *'Do Aankhen Barah Haath'* showed a jailor undertaking to reform six dreaded jail inmates, which was indicative of the importance of the role of jails in the system. Today, jails are shown far from the place of reform but a den of corruption and little has been done to address this situation. Perhaps the only significant example where courts took notice of this fact was when Justice D.Y. Chandrachud directed an enquiry into the condition of the Tihar Jail in a case of blatant misuse of the jail premises by an influential realtor. Needless to say, the results were startling. It was a damning report filed by the Commissioner of Police, Delhi, and the officials were changed overnight. However, on a broader level, does it really change the situation? Perhaps not!

Jail administration needs an overhaul and so do the jail rules which are archaic and far from addressing the present reality. The true meaning of rehabilitation and reform is not being addressed in jails today and steps should be taken to address these issues.

10. Press and Media

Role and Interest

As the fourth pillar of democracy, the press and media play a pivotal role in affecting the opinion and perspective of society. In today's times, internet accessibility has expanded conventional press and media to include social media platforms such as twitter, facebook, and instagram, among others, which have become vehicles to polarize and mobilize people, and resultantly, are powerful tools which have an impact on a section of society.

The press and media may apply pressure and often determine the course and nature of investigation, while also having an impact on the decision-making process of courts. While press and media play an important role in keeping the public informed, a balance needs to be struck between 'informative expression' and 'trial by media'. A responsible media should not let ratings and sensationalism govern their primary responsibility to give an unbiased and factual narrative of a case. The moment the media enters into a mini-trial on its own, it oversteps into the domain of both the investigation and adjudication process.

Rights and Entitlements

The press and media have rights to report on and comment on cases, but they must exercise restraint and be responsible for circulation and distribution of content. Under the present law, there is only an express bar against disclosure of information prohibited by any court of law. All information otherwise can be circulated and distributed, so long as it does not interfere or obstruct the course of justice.

While there are reasonable restrictions placed by the Indian Constitution on the exercise of freedom of speech and expression, 'administration of justice' is not expressly mentioned.

Impact

The societal view of a case is formed by the media coverage, more specifically in today's age. During 'media trials', the accused and their family are unnecessarily scrutinised by the media and every aspect of their personal lives, including aspects which do not pertain to the investigation, are delved into and publicised. This rampant demonisation of the accused violates his fundamental rights and goes against the cornerstone of the criminal justice system, that is, the accused should be treated as an innocent person until proven guilty. Many a time, victims also suffer character assassination at the hands of the media.

In the absence of effective restrictions, as on date, the press and media continue to influence cases and their outcome. Media influence has the tendency of impacting the investigation and the adjudication process, since the pressure to fit into the media narrative becomes immense. Some famous cases of media trials include the *Sushant Singh Rajput* case, the *Priyadarshini Mattoo* case, the *Jessica Lal* case, the *Nitish Katara* case, the *Bijal Joshi* rape case and the *Aarushi Talwar* case.

Need of the Hour

The press and media have their own agendas and narratives. They should not be allowed to influence the other stakeholders for their gain. It is necessary to regulate the press and media by coming up with definitive parameters as to the extent of reporting of cases. While court proceedings are open and the public has a right to know about the cases, sensitivity and a humane approach must be adopted by the press and media while reporting judicial proceedings. This helps not only the accused and the victims but also has a positive impact on the psyche of investigators and the court.

In the *Sahara* case, the power of the courts to prohibit and regulate media reporting was given high importance. The Norms of Journalistic Conduct have also been issued as guidelines for journalists and pertain to ethical and truthful reporting. However, these existing laws require more teeth to prevent irresponsible and unethical reporting.

11. Conclusion

In conclusion, it is evident that each stakeholder has a distinct role and function in the criminal justice system. The interdependence of stakeholders on one another for an efficient functioning of the criminal justice system is also apparent. Thus, if each stakeholder acknowledges the need for effective coordination, performs their duty diligently, and shows responsibility, we can create a robust and strong criminal justice system.

II

INVESTIGATION

1. Introduction

Criminal investigation is one of the most important functions performed by law enforcement agencies in the Indian criminal justice system. The fundamental reason behind this is that an investigation triggers the entire functioning of the criminal justice system and involves the participation of all stakeholders. Without an investigation, there would be no collection of evidence and thus no trial. The criminal justice system's foundation thus rests on a structured and efficient investigating arm which investigates in a meticulous and fair manner. If the investigation is compromised or replete with loopholes, the subsequent trial is adversely impacted, as a result of which justice cannot be meted to either the victim or the accused.

The investigating agency must act responsibly and not infringe upon the rights of either the accused or the victim. It must uphold the edifice of the criminal justice system, that is, transparency, fairness, and justice.

The CrPC defines investigation as the *'collection of evidence'* by a police officer or a magistrate. While the collection of evidence is one of the many functions performed by an investigating agency, the definition does not adequately encompass or reflect all the facets of an investigation. The definition embodied in the CrPC is very restrictive, myopic and static. In actuality, the role of investigating agencies is very broad and diverse. It is not restricted to the mere collection of evidence but also calls upon the investigating agencies to conduct an impartial investigation for ensuring justice. Further, a criminal investigation comprises many stakeholders, as discussed in the previous chapter. All these stakeholders have an impact on the criminal investigation and vice-versa.

Over the years, criminal investigations have become more complex due to evolving technology, increasing presence of the press and media and the growth of social media. The advent of new-age crimes involving multiple jurisdictions and complex transactions has also posed challenges to both, domestic and cross-border collection of evidence by investigating agencies. Further, growth in technology and increased accessibility to the internet has resulted in more engagement of society, including the victim and the accused as well as their families, with criminal investigations. This is a result of regular reporting of cases, especially high-profile cases, and pressure from society to hasten the investigation.

In the light of the above, this chapter will deal with all the different parts and stages of a criminal investigation in India, beginning with the role of the police to the role played by witnesses including the accused and other suspects; the process of registration of cases; search and seizure; attachment and confiscation; arrest, bail and remand; LRs; forensic and medical examination.

2. Role of Police, Witnesses, Accused, Other Suspects (not witnesses)

(A) ROLE OF POLICE

In an investigation in India, the most pivotal role is that of an investigating agency which is either the police or a specialised agency.

First Point of Contact for the Victim

A victim's first brush with the criminal justice system is through the police. As soon as an incident or offence takes place, the victim or the victim's family or any bystander to the incident, calls up the police for assistance. The police is thus the state's first responder to crime, and the first stakeholder to arrive at the crime scene. The role of the police is crucial in this regard. They are the first to record the victim's statement, the first to assess the scene of the crime, and the first to collect primary evidence from the crime scene. Apart from being the victim's first point of contact with the criminal justice system, the police are also the first ones to engage with the accused after apprehending him. They are also the ones to arrest the accused, record his statement and question him about the crime. Even though statements made by accused to the police are *prima facie* inadmissible in court except for grave exceptions under law where the statute provides otherwise, these statements tend to provide a starting point for the investigation.

As soon as the victim or any other person experiences or witnesses a crime, such person can lodge a complaint with the police. Ideally, a complaint should be filed immediately or as soon as possible after a crime occurs. A criminal complaint can be filed by anybody, including the victim's family, friends, bystander, or anybody else, who has witnessed the crime or has knowledge of the same. A complaint can be made by physically going to the police station or through the internet, by filling a form on the police's dedicated website if any, or by writing a letter or disclosing the commission of the offence or through a telephonic call. If the complaint has been filed through the website, the complainant will receive a copy of the complaint filed on the email address. If the complainant goes to the police station, the complainant can orally provide the requisite information and details of the crime to the *munshi* at the police station, who will record the same in the DDR. No legal knowledge or information is necessary and the complaint can be filed in any language. In case the information is given through telephone or any other communication mode, the police is duty bound to act on it and make necessary enquiries from the complainant, should the need be.

Even if the details of the accused are not available, a brief physical description of the accused will suffice for the complaint. No additional documents are required at this stage. Oral information disclosing the commission of a cognizable offence is sufficient to lodge the initial complaint. After the complaint has been recorded, a signed and stamped copy of the complaint is provided to the complainant. Once a complaint is recorded in the DDR, the next step is to lodge the FIR. Once the FIR is lodged, the police officially begin investigation.

Steps of Investigation and Investigator

Under the CrPC, investigation consists of the following steps which are generally undertaken by the police: (1) Proceeding to the spot, (2) Ascertaining facts and circumstances of the case, (3) Discovery and arrest of the suspected offender, (4) Collection of evidence relating to the commission of the offence which may consist of: (a) Examination of various persons, including accused, and the reduction of their statements in writing, if the officer thinks fit, (b) Search of places and seizure of things considered necessary for investigation and are later required to be produced at the stage of trial, and (5) Formation of opinion on whether the material collected is sufficient for placing the accused before the court for trial and, if yes, then filing a charge sheet under S. 173 CrPC.

Primarily, mid-level police officials between the ranks of assistant sub-inspector and deputy superintendent of police lead the investigation. Other senior police officials perform a supervisory role while juniors provide aid and assistance to the officer leading the investigation.

Lack of Uniformity and Challenges

Police and public order are State subjects. Each state has its own DNA and as such a distinct procedure and practice. Resultantly, the nature and manner of investigation in different states has evolved differently. The manner of investigation by the police reflects the society in which the investigation is conducted. Such policies are thus shaped by the society's mindset and perception. Language, dialects, culture and the extant social milieu of the region, all have a considerable impact in shaping the practices of the police. For instance, the manner of conducting investigations in Delhi will be different from that in Maharashtra. The practices also vary from region to region within a state, more specifically amongst the different rural and urban belts.

The lack of training, improper collection of forensic evidence, absence of modernisation and the failure of investigating agencies to keep pace with technology has also impacted the pace and efficiency of investigations in India. The biggest challenges faced by the police and specialised agencies include the lack of uniformity in processes and practices during investigation. In the absence of standardised procedures, the nature and manner of investigation is state-specific rather than statute-specific. This causes confusion and creates substantial impediments in coordination between different agencies and police officers, especially in cross-border investigations involving more than one state. In the absence of a nodal or lead agency, there is overlapping jurisdiction of state police and central agencies. This causes confusion and inter-departmental clashes.

Further, the lack of cultivation and implementation of scientific methods of investigation are major concerns. This can be addressed by upgrading scientific tools and providing police officers with consistent and regular training in the latest methods of investigation.

Limited resources and paucity of investigators in India leading to understaffing results in investigators being overworked and not being able to dedicate considerable time to investigation. This often results in fundamental lapses in investigation and leads to essential evidence getting lost, destroyed, or tampered.

(B) ROLE OF WITNESSES

Meaning of the term 'Witness'

The significance attached to witnesses during investigation in particular, to the criminal justice system as a whole, needs no introduction. An ideal witness is an assistant in the administration of justice, helping not only the prosecution or the defence, but also the court in finding out the truth. He not only clarifies what happened at the crime scene, but also provides other relevant details relating to the offence. Witness testimony is a verbal account of events or knowledge of the facts relevant to the crime.

While in law, witnesses can be classified into more than 30 categories, including eyewitness, material witness, interested witness, injury witness, chance witness, expert witness, accomplice, character witness, child witness, dumb witness, hostile witness, police witness, official witness, and the like, this categorization becomes critical at the stage of trial, when the judge tests the credibility of the witness. At the investigation stage, the witnesses can roughly be classified into the following broad categories:

1. People who are acquainted or know the facts and circumstances of the case are crucial for the investigator to complete the investigation and find the truth. It is the investigator who collects evidence from these people and seeks their help to throw light on the case. Only when the investigator finds it necessary that such a person is essential to prove his case, the statement of such person, recorded during investigation, is made a part of the charge sheet and his name is added to the list of witnesses, which the prosecution proposes to examine during the trial.
2. Investigating Witnesses: These are persons aiding the investigation. Such witnesses, even though possible ones, can be police officials aiding the main investigator, as well as such other departmental and official witnesses summoned by the investigating officer to collect documents. They can also include such persons required by the investigator to comply with the requirements of law during investigation, that is, witnesses of arrest, witnesses of search and seizure, and the like. Such witnesses are generally examined only in court.

It is always the discretion of the investigator to determine the proposed witnesses that he wants to cite in the charge sheet to prove the case of the prosecution. A list of these proposed witnesses is filed along with the charge sheet and comes from either of the above classifications. Even then, for such persons to be treated as a final witness in court, they have to be examined by the prosecutor. Should the prosecutor choose to not examine such people, they do not qualify as witnesses. As such, it is only such people who are examined in court that qualify the definition of a final witness.

Responsibility as an Investigator

As an investigator, it becomes important to firstly identify the persons found as apparent witnesses and get accurate information about their identity. This reduces the risk of losing crucial evidence at a later stage. Once these witnesses are identified, there is a need to assess their credibility. Such an assessment would help in determining if a suspect is posing as a witness. It is not uncommon for a perpetrator to report a crime by posing as a witness or a victim. The investigator must also ensure that the witness on whom he is relying to prove his case is competent to furnish the evidence, that is, the witness is capable of understanding the questions and giving rational answers to them.

Additionally, rules of evidence and protocols must be followed by the investigator for evaluating witnesses and collecting witness evidence that will be acceptable to courts. The statements of witnesses become a part of the case diary and often the charge sheet. The contents of their statements are used by the prosecution for the foundation of its case and to show the credibility of the witnesses. Considering the importance attached to such statements, they should be as accurate and complete as possible to avoid the defence denting the prosecution case. Alternatively, it also helps the court in finding out if the witness is planted or influenced to suit the prosecution case.

Often, citing a long list of witnesses proposed to be examined by the prosecution can be reflective of the prosecution being unsure of its own case. A strategy must be in place to recognize the number of witnesses required since it helps in not only giving a fair idea about the merits of the case but also later facilitates in efficiently conducting the trial.

Treatment of Witness

Since a witness sacrifices his time and effort to provide evidence, he must be given due respect for his service in the administration of justice. Though at the stage of trial, the law mandates payment of allowance and expenses to the witnesses as well as witness protection programmes, such measures have not achieved the desired results. The situation is worse at the stage of investigation. Contrary to being paid due respect and given due comfort, witnesses, or potential witnesses, are ill-treated. They are neither made aware of the details of the case nor given any clarity with respect to their rights, much less their status, at the stage of investigation by the police.

A recent trend in specialized statutes has seen the same mode of summoning people, irrespective of whether they are accused, or suspects or witnesses to the case. As such, on receipt of a summons to join investigation, a person who can be a star witness for the prosecution and help unravel the truth is often scared. This lack of clarity results in the person firstly availing legal help and spending his resources; secondly, attempting to avoid joining investigation and thirdly not coming clean about the case, in turn hampering the investigation of the case.

Despite the law providing for witness statements not being used against them generally, witnesses tend to avoid joining investigations for fear of harassment by the investigating agency, to either suit the narrative of the prosecution or to avoid being made an accused by paying a price. This deters the witness from cooperating with investigations and, as a result, adversely affects the overall sanctity of both, investigation and trial.

Remedial First Step

Importance must be given to the physical or mental vulnerability of the witnesses, and suitable provisions should be made in the criminal justice system at the stage of investigation itself. Without addressing the fear of the public with respect to joining the investigation and changing public perception, an efficient criminal justice system will always remain a distant reality. As a first step, there is a need to inform the witness about the case by sharing adequate details including his status in the case and his rights. With this clarity, the witness would be more comfortable to come forward and cooperate with the investigation. Communication and summons to this effect can be made using the model forms, as enclosed. The said forms not only inform the witness about his legal rights and obligations, but also assist the investigating agency by giving the witnesses a brief background of the case so as to get the most efficient result during the course of their examination.

NAME OF POLICE STATION

(Mention complete address/contact number)

FORM No. [..........]

[See Chapter [.........]]

Dated: ....

Summon to a Witness

[*Kindly note that there shall be 2 Copies carried by the Officer. The signature of the person accepting service of summon and date of such service shall be made on the copy of the Officer. The clear copy shall be given to the person accepting service.*]

FIR No: .... U/s: ....

Reference No: ....

To,

....

(Name & Designation of Person Summoned)

....

(Address of Person Summoned)

Subject: Summon under Section 160 CrPC

The undersigned is conducting an investigation in case FIR No. [..........] P.S. dated [..........]. The brief facts of the case for you to have a background are narrated hereunder:

1. [..........]
2. [..........]

It is the belief of the undersigned that you possess knowledge or information relevant to the case under investigation, [**Optional: as evident from the following**]:

1. [..........]
2. [..........].

For the purposes of aiding the ongoing investigation and in exercise of the powers conferred under Section 160 of the Code of Criminal Procedure, the undersigned requires your attendance [in person/through authorised representative] before him on [..........] at [..........] hours at his office *(Address of Office)*.

The undersigned further requires you/authorized representative to carry and furnish the following documents for the purposes of the investigation, which shall be in [Original/Photocopy/Digitally stored in a storage device (such as pen-drive, hard-drive, etc)]:

S. No.	*Brief Description of the Document required*
	Any other document connected with the case.

Kindly note that in terms of Section 161 of the Code of Criminal Procedure, you are duty bound to state the truth and cooperate with the investigation. Your evidence cannot and will not be used against you and the undersigned extends his gratitude in anticipation of your service to society by cooperating with the investigation, stating the truth and giving all relevant information and material in your possession in relation to the present FIR.

Kindly note that in case of your failure or refusal to appear before the undersigned and/or furnish the documents listed above without reasonable cause communicated to the undersigned, the undersigned is at liberty to initiate proceedings against you under Section 174 Indian Penal Code.

(Signature and Stamp of the Investigating Officer)

NAME OF POLICE STATION
(Mention complete address/contact number)

FORM No. [..........]

[See Chapter [..........]]

Dated: ....

Notice to a Witness

[Kindly note that there shall be 2 Copies carried by the Officer. The signature of the person accepting service of summon and date of such service shall be made on the copy of the Officer. The clear copy shall be given to the person accepting service.]

FIR No: .... U/s: ....

Reference No: ....

To,

....

(Name & Designation of Person Summoned)

....

(Address of Person Summoned)

Subject: Notice under Section 91 CrPC

The undersigned is conducting an investigation in case FIR No. [..........] P.S. dated [..........]. The brief facts of the case for you to have a background are narrated hereunder:

1. [..........]
2. [..........]

It is the belief of the undersigned that you possess knowledge or information relevant to the case under investigation, [**Optional: as evident from the following**]:

1. [..........]
2. [..........].

For the purposes of aiding the ongoing investigation and in exercise of the powers conferred under Section 91 of the Code of Criminal Procedure, the undersigned requires you/authorized representative to [appear before him and] furnish the following documents for the purposes of the investigation before him on [..........] at [..........] hours at his office *(Address of Office)*, which shall be in [Original/Photocopy/Digitally stored in a storage device (such as pen-drive, hard-drive, etc)]:

S. No.	*Brief Description of the Document required*
	Any other document connected with the case.

Kindly note that your evidence cannot and will not be used against you and the undersigned extends his gratitude in anticipation of your service to society by cooperating with the investigation, ***[appearing before the undersigned, if applicable]*** and giving all relevant information and material in your possession in relation to the present FIR.

Kindly note that in case of your failure to ***[appear before the undersigned and, if applicable]*** furnish the documents listed above without reasonable cause communicated to the undersigned, the undersigned is at liberty to initiate proceedings against you under Section 174 Indian Penal Code.

(Signature and Stamp of the Investigating Officer)

(C) ROLE OF ACCUSED

Who is an Accused?

An accused is a person against whom allegations of committing an offence have been made but not yet proved. An accused could be anyone and there are no predefined character traits for labelling a person as an 'accused'. Although the truth of his culpability is decided in due course, today's reality is that the moment a person becomes an accused, his and his family's life dramatically changes for the worse.

The social stigma surrounding an accused and the consequential treatment awarded to an accused and his family is opposed to the scheme of the criminal justice system and its endeavour to ensure accessibility of fairness and justice to one and all. An accused more often than not is a 'victim of circumstances' where he is either the target of malicious accusations which permanently damages his reputation and livelihood, or suffers and is stuck in the rigmarole of the system. This chapter focuses on the rebranding of an accused and the key role of each stakeholder in such process.

Merely becoming an Accused does not make him a criminal

In today's climate, the treatment of an accused during investigation is equivalent to that of a convicted criminal. The stakeholders of the criminal justice system tend to brand and treat an accused as a criminal while forgetting that he is innocent until proved otherwise while also forgetting the strong possibility of an accused being a victim of circumstances. It becomes questionable as to what will be left of the importance accorded to the outcome of investigation and the decision of the courts if we stick to our assumptions and biases with little heed to know the truth. Wouldn't that nullify the existence of the criminal justice system itself and deem it redundant?

It is thus extremely important for each stakeholder to be cautious of their actions and conduct while dealing with an accused. The attitude towards an accused should be one of safeguarding his interests rather than character shaming or demeaning such person. An accused and his family should not be subjected to inhumane treatment, trauma or harassment. The situation as of today must be resolved in a manner where an accused does not think that his and his family's life is over the moment he is involved in a case.

Public Perception: Treatment of Accused

There are many types of accused. Such classification depends on the kind of offence the person is accused of, his societal and economic status and whether he is a first time or habitual offender. An accused could be an adult, child, woman, company, agent of an organisation or a member of the mafia. He may be accused of cognizable of non-cognizable offences, of offences attracting seven years or more imprisonment, of white-collar crimes or of domestic violence cases. He may even be someone falsely implicated in cases, which is rampant in cases of sexual harassment, domestic violence, rape, etc. The perception of an accused must conform to the various shades of an accused and there cannot be a uniform treatment for all types of accused.

The treatment of an accused also varies with the kind of cases that are causing concern in society. For example, earlier there were rampant crimes involving dowry deaths and the treatment of accused of dowry deaths was at that time very different from their treatment now where dowry deaths have reduced and law enforcement authorities recognize the possibility of false allegations in these cases. Cases of cheating, criminal breach of trust, forgery and the likes are now increasing. The law enforcement authorities and courts are enforcing stricter measures on accused in such cases.

It is important to recognize that all accused persons cannot be perceived or treated alike. The law also differentiates between the types of accused, and each stakeholder must understand such difference. Such differentiation is critical since the treatment by different stakeholders changes the life of a person. Such treatment has a grave bearing on the accused as well as his family's livelihood, stature in society and their future.

How does Victim see an Accused?

For a victim or the victim's family, the accused is a criminal. Whether or not the complaint is *bona fide* or the accused is proven innocent or guilty, the victim/victim's family will always hold the accused accountable. This is the simple reason to have intermediaries such as the police and courts in the system so as to give the accused a fair chance to defend himself, and for the police and the courts to sieve through the exaggerations, lies, or any misunderstandings of the victim in order to discover the truth.

How does an Investigator see an Accused?

An accused interacts with various stakeholders at different stages. His very first interaction is with the investigator, who not only shapes the foundation of the case but also sets the pattern for treatment of an accused by other stakeholders.

The stage of investigation allows an interaction between the accused and the investigator, where the investigator can seek information from an accused during investigation. This presents an opportunity for the accused to come forward, justify himself and deflect any apprehensions or suspicions that have been levelled against him at the initial stage. This also enables the investigator to understand whether the accused is a victim of circumstances, the degree of his complicity in the offence and whether the accused is cooperating with the investigation or is being evasive. It is on the basis of such understanding that the investigator decides to arrest, take custody of the accused, provide inputs on his release of bail, etc.

The law even prescribes the standards which an investigator must maintain in his treatment of an accused. An investigator is strictly discouraged from using excessive force or illegal means in his treatment of an accused. The law also recognises that an accused may be subject to undue pressure or threat to reveal information or be forced to accept false facts or evidence. In such cases, he has the right to speak against such arbitrary, unfair or unreasonable treatment and the courts are duty bound to protect his rights.

How do Courts see an Accused?

The courts have always laid emphasis on the fair and just treatment of accused while also ensuring that the accused does not act contrary to the process of law. The courts weigh the requirements of an investigation while curtailing the liberty of an accused and in doing so, reinforce the difference in treatment between the various types of accused.

The unique treatment of each accused is upheld by the courts. Logically, an accused of a marital dispute or cheque bouncing case or traffic violations cannot surely be put into the shoes of an accused who has committed heinous crimes or serious offences attracting life imprisonment or capital punishment. Even the law differentiates between an accused committing a cognizable or non-cognizable crime and prescribes a different procedure and standard of assessment under each type of crime, which is duly followed by the courts. Many judicial pronouncements in the past have also sought to establish the treatment of an accused by taking into account his background, the type of accused he may be, and the circumstances of the case.

How do Press and Media see an Accused?

The information disseminated by the press and media, although meant to keep the public informed and aware, can negatively affect the outcome of an investigation. Their views deeply influence society and, in turn, could prejudice the investigator and the justice system, which are also a part of society. The media sometimes generalises all kinds of accused into one box which could impact the manner an accused is dealt with. It is crucial to verify the credibility and authenticity of information. There should be restraint in sharing any irrelevant or unnecessary information and the media should allow investigation to take its own course without tainting the public's trust and faith in the state machinery. Thus, the media's treatment of an accused must be confined to only relevant and unbiased reporting. The impact of the media can be long lasting and cause permanent damage which will ultimately hinder the reintegration of an accused into society, even after exoneration.

How does Society see an Accused?

Society often brands an accused as a criminal and chooses to distance itself from those involved in any kind of investigations or complaints. The accused and his family are often isolated and removed from jobs, neighbourhoods, schools, colleges, etc. The instant reaction of society towards an accused and his family subjects them to social exile and punishment. Over the years, with the evolution of law and general awareness of rights, society is slowly reassessing its definition of an accused which is a welcome step.

Rights of an Accused during Investigation

The rights of an accused during investigation emanate from the Indian Constitution, the CrPC and precedents. Broadly, the fundamental right to life guaranteed under Article 21 of the Constitution of India grants the accused a right to represent himself before courts through a lawyer of his choice and also have free and fair access to justice. An accused also has the right to protect himself from divulging any information that may incriminate him, that is, right against self-incrimination. The protection extends to instances which may expose the accused to charges other than those for which he is suspected or formally charged. This right further includes the right to silence and the right to refuse Deception Detection Tests (DDT). An accused also has the right to have a lawyer of his choice during interrogation in custody and to be protected from custodial torture.

Building Faith in the System

Keeping illegalities of investigation aside, the accused needs guidance on how to face investigative agencies when he is summoned for questioning or asked for information. He must not run from pillar to post in frenzy and live in fear just because he has received a notice or summons. He must understand that he is being called to play a part in the investigation and cannot in any way be made to suffer just because he is an accused. He must be given such reassurance by the police or investigative agencies. The basic step towards ensuring the same is by making it mandatory for the investigator to spell out in his summons the reason for asking a person to join the investigation and in what capacity, what are the allegations against him or what is the subject of the investigation and what information is exactly required from such person being called. For this purpose, it is advised that all investigative agencies should prepare a questionnaire that informs the accused of what is needed from him. This will help give the accused clarity about the case and also facilitate an effective exchange of information and progress in investigation. The accused would also gain confidence in the system and not unnecessarily panic before joining an investigation.

(D) OTHER SUSPECTS (NOT WITNESSES)

Who is a Suspect?

A suspect is considered as a likely offender and is a potential accused. The suspect may be someone not known or named in the FIR itself, and not clearly visible at the stage when the crime is reported. Another category of suspects can be someone named in the FIR, but there being doubts about the possibility of such person committing the crime. A suspect is as such someone who is under suspicion of committing an offence and is one-step away from becoming an accused.

Where the case has civil connotations and till the time the ingredients and intention are not considered to be that of a crime, a person is a suspect. Suspects are also made in cases where there is an exaggeration with respect to involvement of people by the complainant, that is, where a number of persons are impleaded in a violent case or dowry case; where the entire family is roped in; or any case where there is a telltale sign of an exaggerated claim or involvement of people. Thus, instead of making all such persons accused, police brands those persons as suspects against whom there are half baked or unsure allegations. During investigation, as and when information is received, the investigator could grow speculative of the involvement of other potential accused and choose to investigate such persons. In case the suspect does not turn out to be an accused, he can still prove to be an excellent witness for the prosecution.

Treatment of Suspects

Since a suspect is neither an accused nor a witness, this lack of clarity leaves the suspect confused and magnifies his fear towards being treated like an accused by the police. When a suspect joins an investigation, he must also be made aware of his rights and duties. His treatment by an investigator should be in his capacity of a suspect and not an accused. Suspicions regarding his role, the information he gives and the extent of his knowledge must be tested in order for the investigator to decide his status as to whether he is an accused, or a witness or has no role in the case.

To address these concerns, as a first step, each suspect should be informed about his status as a suspect and not made an accused as yet. Giving such clarity helps suspects understand why they are being called by the police for investigation and in what capacity. This is also important to prevent suspects from running to court, fearing that they are being prosecuted and could be arrested. Sample forms which could be issued by the police or investigating authorities, clarifying the status of a suspect, are given below.

Notice of Arrest

The day the investigator decides to arrest a suspect, he must immediately inform the suspect of such impending arrest by way of a notice which must clearly state the reasons for such arrest. This gives time to the suspect to seek any legal remedy or make necessary arrangements for his arrest and ensuing events post arrest. In cases where the investigator feels that urgent action must be taken against the suspect and there is no time to send the notice of arrest, which will only alert the suspect to flee, tamper with evidence or influence witnesses, then the investigator can refrain from sending such notice with his reasons in writing. However, these reasons must be later tested by the courts to see whether they were reasonable. If found that the investigator has overreached and the reasons fail to stand the scrutiny of the court, action must be taken against the erring official along with compensation given to the suspect for his illegal arrest, more specifically since the officer was within his rights to impose reasonable restrictions to secure the presence of the said individual.

Treatment of Suspects and their Rights

Due to the unique nature of a suspect, the investigation should be equipped with safeguards for protecting the interests of the suspect. Over the years, judicial decisions have provided some insight into the rights available to a suspect at the time of an investigation. A suspect is protected under Article 20(3) of the Constitution of India during a criminal investigation. He has a right to refuse to answer questions which might expose him to a criminal charge and not undergo DDTs.

We should be cautious that the suspect does not become a tool in the hand of the investigator and then used in a manner prejudicial to justice. In a plethora of cases across India, suspects are used as puppets during investigation. There is a sword looming over the suspect and he is scared to become an accused, thus mischievously stating false and exaggerated facts to deflect suspicion. Suspects are sometimes used by the police to knit together false and fabricated facts to attribute guilt to the accused. Thus, statements and information given by suspects cannot always be trusted and the testimonies should not blindly be used to corroborate the evidence against an accused.

Similarly, like the accused, the suspect has a right to a just and fair investigation. The investigator should be fair, conscious and impartial while dealing with a suspect. Further, the suspect has a right against third degree methods of interrogation. Where any hurt or grievous hurt is caused to a suspect with the intent to extort a confession or compel restoration of property, then remedies under the IPC are available to him. A suspect is also given the same rights during arrest, search and seizure as that of an accused and all procedural safeguards in this regard are applicable to him.

Need for Securing the Interest and Protection of Suspects during Investigation

Due to the lack of codified guidelines for investigation of suspects, proper interrogation modules should be framed in this regard and must cover every aspect in detail. Strict adherence to these modules should be ensured. Further, suspects should be given relevant information about the interrogation. They should be duly informed regarding the rights and benefits available to them. It must be made imperative for the investigator to inform the suspect about his rights under law. Similar provisions should be made to uphold the suspect's right to attain all material information about the investigation. This right should be extended to also inform the suspect of when he becomes an accused, so that he has an opportunity to exercise his rights as an accused. This will ensure a fair investigation to the suspect, free from any personal bias or other influences of the investigator.

NAME OF POLICE STATION

(Mention complete address/contact number)

FORM No. [..........]

[See Chapter [..........]]

Dated: ....

Summon to a Suspect

[Kindly note that there shall be 2 Copies carried by the Officer. The signature of the person accepting service of summon and date of such service shall be made on the copy of the Officer. The clear copy shall be given to the person accepting service.]

FIR No: .... U/s: ....

Reference No: ....

To,

....

(Name & Designation of Person Summoned)

....

(Address of Person Summoned)

Subject: Summon under Section 160 CrPC

The undersigned is conducting an investigation in case FIR No. [..........] P.S. dated [..........]. The brief facts of the case for you to have a background are narrated hereunder:

1. [..........]
2. [..........]

You are a suspect in the case under investigation, **[Optional: as evident from the following]**:

1. [..........]
2. [..........].

For the purposes of aiding the ongoing investigation and in exercise of the powers conferred under Section 160 of the Code of Criminal Procedure, 1973 the undersigned requires your attendance [in person/ through authorised representative] before him on [..........] at [..........] hours at his office _(Address of Office)_.

The undersigned further requires you/authorized representative to carry and furnish the following documents for the purposes of the investigation, which shall be in [Original/ Photocopy/Digitally stored in a storage device (such as pen-drive, hard-drive, etc)]:

S. No.	*Brief Description of the Document required*
	Any other document connected with the case.

Kindly note that in terms of Section 161 of the Code of Criminal Procedure, 1973 you are duty bound to state the truth and cooperate with the investigation. Your evidence cannot and will not be used against you. The undersigned sincerely hopes that you will come clean about your role in the case, state the truth and give all relevant information and material in your possession in relation to the present FIR.

Kindly note that in case of your failure or refusal to appear before the undersigned and/or furnish the documents listed above without reasonable cause communicated to the undersigned, the undersigned is at liberty to initiate proceedings against you under Section 174 of the Indian Penal Code, 1860.

(Signature and Stamp of the Investigating Officer)

NAME OF POLICE STATION

(Mention complete address/contact number)

FORM No. [..........]

[See Chapter [..........]]

Dated: ....

Notice to a Suspect

[Kindly note that there shall be 2 Copies carried by the Officer. The signature of the person accepting service of summon and date of such service shall be made on the copy of the Officer. The clear copy shall be given to the person accepting service.]

FIR No: .... U/s: ....

Reference No: ....

To,

....

(Name & Designation of Person Summoned)

....

(Address of Person Summoned)

Subject: Notice under Section 91 CrPC

The undersigned is conducting an investigation in case FIR No. [..........] P.S. dated [..........]. The brief facts of the case for you to have a background are narrated hereunder:

1. [..........]
2. [..........]

You are a suspect in the case under investigation, [**Optional: as evident from the following**]:

1. [..........]
2. [..........].

For the purposes of aiding the ongoing investigation and in exercise of the powers conferred under Section 91 of the Code of Criminal Procedure, 1973 the undersigned requires you/authorized representative to ***[appear before him and, if applicable]*** furnish the following documents for the purposes of the investigation before him on [..........] at [..........] hours at his office *(Address of Office)*, which shall be in [Original/Photocopy/ Digitally stored in a storage device (such as pen-drive, hard-drive, etc)]:

S. No.	*Brief Description of the Document required*
	Any other document connected with the case.

Kindly note that your evidence cannot and will not be used against you and the undersigned sincerely hopes that you will cooperate with the investigation and give all relevant information and material in your possession in relation to the present FIR.

Kindly note that in case of your failure to ***[appear before the undersigned and, if applicable]*** furnish the documents listed above without reasonable cause communicated to the undersigned, the undersigned is at liberty to initiate proceedings against you under Section 174 of the Indian Penal Code, 1860.

(Signature and Stamp of the Investigating Officer)

3. Registration of a Case

The first important step to put into action the criminal justice system is the registration of a case, which has far-reaching consequences on the trial. When I joined the profession, I was told by experienced lawyers that an FIR is one document which no matter how many times is read will never be sufficient. The best defence lawyers agree with vehemence. The FIR is something which is very sanguine and significant but is treated casually and callously.

Since the registration of a case is being discussed, the ground reality is that a common man finds it difficult to understand how a case is registered. The police in our country has worked very hard to create a fear psychosis amongst the general public, which consequently, is most reluctant to approach the police. So as to speak of consistency, the police is working harder with every passing day to maintain the hype of such fear in the mind of the general public. The fear of being harassed is as much in the mind of the complainant as it is perhaps in the mind of the accused. On paper, it remains a different matter that the police slogan is of being citizen friendly, that is, '*With You, For You Always....*'

Mode of Recording of FIR

At the Police Station

The law mandates the FIR to be recorded on the basis of the complaint by the officer-in-charge of the police station. However, for all practical purposes, it is the *munshi* (clerk of the level of head constable) who generally transcribes the FIR. He enquires about the events from the complainant, draws a sketch of the sequence of events, asks for the number of people that complainant would like to involve and provides the names of such persons who can stand witness. The outcome is a version which is far from the truth and reality. This practice has been assailed through various pronouncements by the apex court.

Additionally, there is a tendency amongst the SHOs and even the *munshis* to ask the informants to bring in written complaints rather than acting on oral complaints, which is contrary to law. This practice is a result of the police mindset to record such written versions which may be easily proved and accepted by the court.

At the Scene of Crime

In cases where the complainant does not go to the police station but where the police reach the spot or where the investigator reaches the hospital, the effort on the part of the investigator is to record the FIR on the statement of an injured only, who at times is not even fit to make that statement. The investigator has to wait for the injured person to be declared fit. Such delays can be fatal for the case and cases can be dismissed on the delay in lodging the FIR. These delays can be avoided if the investigator records the statement of any other person accompanying the injured and well conversant with the facts of the case.

At the Instance of a Lawyer

When the above situations are absent, another wonderful instrument of our criminal justice system is resorted to: a lawyer. His prudence is applied in laying out a plan to involve the maximum people to leave no lacunae in the case. Such a version is then believed to be sacrosanct. What an irony!

On Directions of Court

The wisdom of the court under S. 156(3) CrPC has been made to be used as a tool for the registration of a case, thanks to the pronouncements of the Supreme Court in *Madhu Bala* and *Sakiri Vasu* to act as a check on the police who refuse the registration of FIRs. Such mandates have the tendency of becoming a source of corruption in the police and lower judiciary. The situation has been further aggravated with the apex court directing the mandatory registration of FIRs in all cognizable offences in the case of *Lalita Kumari*, without any verification as to the contents of the complaints. With such unverified allegations being taken on face-value for the registration of FIRs, cases are bound to fall in the courts, resulting in a high acquittal and low conviction rate.

Preliminary Enquiry

A preliminary enquiry is engrained in the process of law and is a practice which must be encouraged. In case of uncertainty regarding commission of an offence, cognizable or non-cognizable, and to deprecate the practice of mechanically registering FIRs, a preliminary enquiry proves rather useful. Besides, at first glance, commission of offences reaches the authorities only by word of mouth and such information should be ascertained as a precursor before registration of a FIR, which has serious consequences.

Lalita Kumari's case has settled the position of law with respect to mandatory registration of FIRs by the police in all complaints disclosing cognizable offences. The court has mandated a preliminary enquiry to be done by the police if the information does not disclose a cognizable offence. Some of the common cases for preliminary enquiry, as tabulated by the apex court, involve family disputes, commercial cases, medical negligence cases, cases where there is a delay in filing a complaint, as well as corruption cases. The court also tried to curb the callous attitude of police officials and mandated that all information relating to cognizable offences, whether resulting in FIRs or leading to a preliminary enquiry, must be mandatorily and meticulously reflected in the DDR, along with the decision to conduct the preliminary inquiry. However, while doing so, the apex court failed to consider the consequences of passing such a blanket order and departed from a better system in place, which system continues to work for the CBI.

The concept of a preliminary enquiry is nothing new. It is rather ingrained in the process of the registration of the case. S. 154 CrPC, which directs the registration of an FIR on the receipt of information relating to the commission of cognizable offence, must be interpreted to safeguard this provision from being used as a tool to harass individuals. Prudence says that to prevent the indiscriminate registration of FIRs on the basis of false complaints, a preliminary enquiry must be done by the police. Such an enquiry, being time bound as per the case of *Lalita Kumari,* would ensure that system is not set in motion as a tool for harassment and for suiting personal gains.

Registration of a case is not a great thing and harassment meted out in the guise of investigation should not become a norm. Under the present law, police is not to generally conduct a preliminary enquiry whereas, in earlier times, such an exercise used to take shape in the form of local policemen resolving quarrels in the neighbourhood by understanding the solution then and there, without registering any FIR. Such an approach further inculcates the practice of mediation and conciliation by resolving petty issues without the necessity of registration of a case. Not only does this save precious judicial time, it also reduces the burden on the state machinery.

Fashion Crimes

A perusal of the statistics of the National Crime Records Bureau would reveal how the nature of crime has evolved over the decades. The first National Crime Records Bureau Report of 1953 shows cases of theft, house breaking and murder as the most prominent crimes being registered. Such a situation continued throughout the 1950s and 1960s, though by the end of the 1950s, cases of rioting, criminal breach of trust and cheating started to significantly increase in number.

In the 1970s, incidents of dacoity and robbery saw a significant increase, while incidents of murder saw a slow curve till the mid-1970s. Additionally, offences under the Prohibition Act, Gambling Act and Excise Act gained prominence and this situation continued throughout the 1970s.

The 1980s saw a significant increase in the cases of rape, murder, homicide, rioting, kidnapping, robbery and cheating. With the enactment of the Commission of Sati (Prevention) Act, the decade also saw significant cases of *sati* and suicide coming to light.

With the 1990s opening up the Indian economy to the world, violent crimes like murder, burglary, riots and robbery saw a decline. However, cases of theft and cheating rapidly increased. The biggest change during the 1990s was the quantification and tabulation of crimes against women, showing rape, torture, kidnapping, dowry death and molestation cases increasing, which was also a result of the empowerment of women finally showing results.

When the courts eventually started realizing how dowry cases were being misused, the early 2000s saw a new trend of cases of cruelty being filed, not only against the husband, but also against the family members of the husband. It was much later in 2014 that the Supreme Court put a strict stop to the misuse of these cases by mandating both a reference to mediation as well as bail in all such cases. Over a period of time, the cruelty cases saw a sharp decline.

Once the cases of cruelty lost teeth, a recent trend of rape cases on the pretext of marriage, unnatural sex, outraging the modesty of women or marital rape gained prominence in the last decade. Separately, the cases against real estate players picked up tremendously in the last decade. This is peculiar since there is no material change in the housing practices since the early 2000s. While there was very little or no discontent against these builders earlier, the cases have since increased exponentially since the civil remedies and specialized tribunals like the RERA and consumer forums have failed to address the grievances effectively. Any efforts undertaken by them was perhaps too little too late. The misuse of public money by realtors and the courts coming down heavily on such incidents led to an unprecedented number of cases of cheating, criminal breach of trust, forgery and falsification of accounts being filed. However, the realtors, more often than not, prefer to serve their sentence and escape liability, providing very little respite to homebuyers.

On another front, financial mismanagement and siphoning of government funds first led to the government adding teeth to the powers of the SEBI. Thereafter, the Enforcement Directorate was armed with the Prevention of Money Laundering Act, 2002. More recently, the Black Money and the Benami Transactions Act, as well as the Companies Act 2013 empowering the Serious Fraud Investigation Office, have been brought in to deal with white-collar crimes.

The last decade has in fact seen the maximum number of white-collar cases coming to light, more specifically since the UPA-II regime. While the CBI was earlier dealing with special crimes and only a few corruption cases, there are now dedicated and multiple units in the agency to tackle banking frauds, corruption and economic cases. The central agencies under the specialized statutes are now in a lead role to deal with these white-collar crimes and the state police forces have receded into the background. The recent fall of the Sahara Group has also seen an unprecedented number of cases being investigated by the SEBI while the money laundering investigations are at an all-time high. The downside is critical, but the author refrains from sounding too critical.

As such, different decades and time periods would show how different kinds of cases take priority at the relevant time, which may be politically driven, or a result of the pressure from media, society, social changes, or such other parameters.

Consequences and Features of Registration of FIRs

In addition to the investigation, more importantly, the registration of a case leads to some typical features which are worth pondering over:

1. Indiscriminate mentioning of various sections of offences entails different consequences. Mere mentioning of sections has a bearing on the custody period and bail of the accused.
2. Threat of registration of a case can become a source of corruption in the police. It has been seen that registration of a case has been used to recover money which otherwise is a civil dispute. The power may also be adversely utilized to extort monies and other valuable property at the instance of an enemy of the person arrested.
3. When a cognizable offence is added to a non-cognizable case, the FIR comes into being although ordinarily only a complaint would lie against such offences. Of course, the credit for this innovation goes largely to the investigating agencies, with some support from lawyers. The duty of the investigator is not merely to bolster a prosecution case with evidence as may enable the court to record a conviction but rather to bring out the real unvarnished truth. Although legal history has been reiterated time and again that the police is not to present a draconian picture of its efficiency and working but be citizen-friendly, there has been a sacrilege of this institution of governance.
4. The import of various judgments of the courts gives a right to the victim and, or complainant for registration of the FIR in cases involving cognizable offences, leaving absolutely no space for the police to exercise the discretion in appropriate cases. Even if a magistrate does not say it in so many words while directing

investigation under S. 156 (3) CrPC that the FIR should be registered, it is the duty of the officer in-charge of the police station to register the FIR.

5. It has been so often noticed that a case against an affluent person is registered instantly while cases involving indigents are viewed as a burden. It does not require deep thinking to know the reason behind the same. However, there is the other side of the coin which shows that many a time, affluent people avoid registration of a case or use the police to harass a person who otherwise is wronged but is not from a privileged section of society or does not have access to political power wielders. Sometimes, he can even be made an accused although ideally, in a strict sense of legal ambit, he should have been a complainant.
6. Registration of a case is the rule today but was not so earlier. There was a very healthy practice of recording a DDR entry, holding a preliminary enquiry thereafter, satisfying oneself about the authenticity of the complaint and only then registering the FIR. A vast majority of cases which were not heinous could be resolved with the fair and friendly attitude of police and more importantly, the practice lessened the pressure on the courts and the investigating agencies alike, while also promoting brotherhood in society.
7. As is always the case, a healthy tradition was abused by the police and the affluent, also inducing corruption. However, if we compare this drawback with the advantages mentioned above, the positives that are offered outweigh the negatives. Perhaps, all we need is good and friendly policing and not the dictatorial laws and cumbersome procedures.

Balancing the Act

One must remember that the approach of police is generally different from that of courts. The former is concerned with the result and not with the procedural safeguards and fairness, which have been frowned upon by the Supreme Court. This syndrome of policemen committing crimes and making up perfect paperwork should not be ruled out when courts examine rival versions. While the flip side is bound to be profound, we must not forget that we can still walk around fearlessly after sunset unlike many other countries including America. It is time that frivolous prosecutions, initiated solely to suit personal gains must not be permitted to be launched, even if this results in a miniscule percentage of genuine cases suffering.

Model Setup

1. Whenever a crime is reported or a complaint made, a DDR entry should be made immediately to avoid any allegation of delay.
2. Post this entry, a mandatory preliminary enquiry should be launched to find out if the complaint has some substance, on the basis of which an FIR can be registered. Such an act would keep a check on the indiscriminate registration of cases, having the capacity to cause irreparable harm to the reputation of an individual.
3. For all complaints concerning family disputes, commercial cases, medical negligence, corruption, parking and nuisance disputes, or offences which are otherwise compoundable, a preliminary enquiry must be mandated, during which time, the parties must be encouraged to explore the possibility of settlement in all compoundable offences.
4. Practice of arbitrarily resorting to S. 156(3) CrPC should be discouraged as in almost all the cases, the complaint is a coloured version.
5. The investigation should be fair and impartial. Evidence that favours the accused should be collected and the accused should be informed about it, as done in the American criminal justice system.
6. Exaggerations in the FIR with respect to involving innocent persons at the behest of the complainant should be discouraged. This can be effectively achieved by conducting the preliminary enquiry to ascertain the genuineness of the complaint.
7. Police should be given more liberty to handle the situation at the time of registration of a case. However, if this liberty is misused, the officer should be proceeded against strictly both according to the rules of the department and as per the provisions of the law of the land.
8. Police officers who are seemingly hand in glove with accused should

be penalized for misdemeanour. If such finding of his unruly conduct is clear, disciplinary proceedings should be conducted as a part of the same trial of offence against an accused. A magistrate at the stage of discharge may prosecute the erring official with the complainant under S. 182 IPC and such other offences and proceed further with the inquiry and trial, instead of ordering a fresh investigation.

9. A practice should be evolved to involve respected and responsible individuals of society in the investigation of cases involving the social fabric like dowry, women-related issues and family disputes, to lend more credibility to the genuineness of claim.
10. Matrimonial disputes including domestic violence and divorce cases, for example, involve mediation and, or counselling sessions prior to registration of a case. On similar lines, where statute permits, talks of settlement or compensation should be encouraged in order to reduce the requirement of unnecessary litigations. Alternative Dispute Resolution techniques can serve such purpose. Even if the case is registered, the court can find ways to order Alternative Dispute Resolution if they are sought in appropriate cases, promote initiation of settlement talks and permit withdrawal of cases where the statute so permits, more specifically for offences mentioned in S. 320 CrPC.
11. To deter frivolous cases being filed, a new system can be evolved wherein the police official, the complainant, and the witnesses are all put to stand the test of trial. Should the magistrate find their conduct to be *mala fide* or wanting, they can be prosecuted for fabricating evidence, launching false prosecution and such other offences in the course of the same trial, while also compensating the alleged accused. Such a step would not only reduce the registration of cases by at least 50 per cent, another 25 per cent cases would see closure or lesser number of accused by the police itself, clearing the way for justice in genuine cases.
12. In the fashion crimes mentioned above, such deterrence must be stricter and an amendment for the same purpose can be brought in law.

4. Arrest, Custody, Bail and Remand

Meaning of Arrest

Arrest means deprivation of liberty of a person or confinement by a legal authority. An arrest can be effected by the police and the courts alike. In certain circumstances, even an individual can effect an arrest.

Necessity and pre-requisites of Arrest

1. Besides being dreadful, another feature of arrest is that if it is not a necessity and thus the flexibility and discretion to arrest the accused has the potential of an indiscriminate and arbitrary use of the power of arrest.
2. The apex court in 1994 in *Joginder Kumar's* case observed that arrest is not necessary and should be resorted to only in rare cases when the circumstances so warrant. It would be prudent for a police officer in the interest of protection of the rights of a citizen, and perhaps in his own interest, that no arrest should be made without reaching a reasonable satisfaction after some investigation vis-à-vis the genuineness and *bona fides* of a complaint and reasonable belief of both, the person's complicity as well as the need to effect an arrest.
3. Years later, the Supreme Court in 2014 in *Arnesh Kumar's* case mandated that for any or all offences punishable with imprisonment of up to 7 years, no automatic arrest can be made by the police officer. Only on failing to comply with a notice or in rare cases can an arrest be made, post recording of reasons necessitating such arrest.
4. While the law on paper makes for perfect reading, the corruption and blatant misuse of powers by the police still does not stop. In *Joginder Kumar's* case, there was a reference to the 3rd report of the National Police Commission where it was found that more than 60 per cent of the arrests are unnecessary and are as such a huge burden on the state exchequer, resulting in a staggering 43.2 per cent of prison expenditure. The police is often seen using powers

to summon a person and then abusing the powers in effecting an arrest.

There are so many conferences which are graced by senior judges, senior lawyers, and human rights activists wherein it is generally accepted without any hitch that the police abuses its power of arrest. Even the higher courts are well aware of the situation but still nothing concrete has been done, except for a few stray incidents of contempt proceedings. In most seminars and forums, a perfunctory job of highlighting the horrendous effects of abuse of this power is done. However, this mere lip service cannot and will not lead anywhere. The existence of power to arrest is one thing and justification for the same is quite another. However, the irony is in case the police does not arrest somebody, it is the courts that question them about the reasons for not arresting the accused.

Rights of an Arrested Person

The apex court, in the case of *D.K. Basu*, has laid down the mandatory conditions to be followed during the time of arrest, which have since majorly been incorporated in the CrPC. The following requirements have been mandated to be followed in all cases:

1. The police officer carrying out the arrest shall prepare an arrest memo at the time of arrest, which shall be attested by at least one witness. It shall also be counter-signed by the arrestee and shall contain the time and date of arrest.
2. An arrested person being held in custody is entitled, if he so requests, to have one friend or relative or other person who is known to him or likely to take an interest in his welfare, told as far as practicable that he has been arrested and where he is being detained, unless the attesting witness of the memo is himself such a friend or a relative of the arrestee.
3. The police officer shall inform the arrested person when he is brought to the police station of this right.
4. An entry shall be required to be made in the Diary as to who was informed of the arrest.
5. The arrestee should, where he so requests, be also examined at the

time of his arrest and major and minor injuries, if any present on his body, must be recorded at that time.

6. The arrestee must be subjected to medical examination by a trained doctor every 48 hours.
7. Copies of all the documents including the memo of arrest should be sent to the *Illaqa* Magistrate for his record.
8. The arrestee must be produced before the *Illaqa* Magistrate within 24 hours of arrest.
9. The arrestee may be permitted to meet his lawyer during interrogation, though not throughout the interrogation.

Even though the apex court says that it would be contempt of court if above guidelines are not followed in letter and spirit, courts often ignore such guidelines, hardly taking notice of any indiscriminate or arbitrary arrest which is brought before them. An endeavour must be made against erring policemen for unnecessary arrests. The situation however is such that either all arrests are genuine or the system wants to close its eyes to the arbitrary use of power of arrest. While the writ of *habeas corpus* is a powerful tool to curb any illegal arrest, the mechanical manner of passing remand orders by magistrates has effectively nullified this remedy, since the Supreme Court has barred issuing any such writ post a judicial order remanding the accused to custody.

Custody

Arrest precedes custody. When a person is arrested, he is taken into custody, which custody is then regulated by law. A person arrested cannot be detained for more than 24 hours, post which time, the detention in custody can only be on court orders. When the person is produced before the court, it has the option to either remand him to police custody or judicial custody. However, police custody is restricted to only the first 15 days in remand, be it through one remand order, or through repeated remand orders. Any detention whatsoever post the first 15 days of arrest is only in judicial custody.

As far as the period of judicial custody is concerned, the maximum period for such custody during investigation cannot exceed 60 days or 90 days for offences punishable with less than 10 years and all other offences, respectively. An additional time period is provided under special statutes, which period is generally 180 days for the completion of an investigation. Any lapse on the part of the investigating agency to file a charge sheet during this period leads to a default bail of the accused, which can even be granted on an oral application, and it is also the duty of the judge to inform the accused of such right. The grant of default bail is not on the merits of the case but is primarily a statutory and technical right. However, once a charge sheet is filed within the mandated time period, the right to default bail stands extinguished, and the person is remanded to judicial custody post cognizance.

While the law mandates that each day of police remand must be on the basis of strong reasons warranting such remand, we find that more often than not that both the police as well as judicial remand is extended by the magistrate in a mechanical manner.

I find it pertinent to mention here one such practice adopted by the Punjab and Haryana High Court to expedite bail applications in cases where there the accused may suffer due to no or ineffective legal representation. The judges of the High Court would inspect jails, personally visit the applicants, hear the matter which needed immediate attention, and give a chance to the State and pass orders for grant/refusal of bail. Such pro-active measures and innovative practices should be adopted by states across the country.

Harsh Reality Leading to Custody

With the accused having no access to the case diary, police can write anything in it and come before the magistrate to seek police custody. Very rarely in my 32 years of practice as a lawyer on the criminal side have I come across a judge who refused police custody. All such averments and allegations attributed to the accused for remand often do not form a part of the charge sheet. Such allegations are generally to sensationalize the case, for example by attributing the ghastly crime to an accused who is remotely connected to it or attributing a huge financial crime to a person responsible for a miniscule amount in the entire case.

In most cases, the magistrate decides on the side of the prosecution and lacks in probing or delving deeper into the merits of the allegations. They invariably grant custody which may be grossly abused in harassing the accused. Every moment in police custody is at a premium, having grave implications and wide ramifications on the life of an accused person, his reputation as well as his self-esteem. An eventual acquittal does little to take away the torture in custody while the procrastination of trial shatters his self-image and social presence.

A commonly quoted reason for police custody is custodial interrogation. Does it mean that under the garb of granting police custody, courts tend to justify third degree custodial torture? While the Supreme Court expects the police to act responsibly, the ground reality is to the contrary.

Today, the social scenario vis-à-vis the police force is of fear, awe and apprehension. As compared to the police forces in the West where a five-year-old child would call a police man to help him cross the road, in this country, a five-year-old would cringe and hide behind his mother on spotting a policeman. Such is the rapport our police has built with the general public.

The Unspoken Loss of Man-hours

One arrest, apart from taking away the liberty of the individual, also consumes the time of the arrestee and the arresting officer and the entire state machinery. Immediately on arrest, the family members and friends rush to the police station. The arrestee is then taken to the hospital, again utilizing the services of a doctor and at least two policemen. The arrestee is then produced before court. The magistrate, the PP, the court staff, defence counsels, family members, sureties, and all such participants are made to spend their resources and time on remand proceedings.

The magistrate thereafter remands the accused to custody, be it police or judicial. In either scenario, the entire lock up machinery or jail machinery is put to test, and an over-burdened system is further overloaded. This cycle of remand is repeated with each production.

Surely, a bail application is moved, which is then taken up by the court and notice is issued to the prosecution. Not only does the PP spend his time preparing this reply, the arresting officer and his superiors also spend their time assisting in finalization of the reply. More often than not, the magistrate declines bail at the early stage of investigation, either as a part of his bounden duty or for the fear of higher judiciary. It is very hard to say and harder to write it in print but the apathy of the police and the attitude of the court at the magistracy level is beyond comprehension.

The bail application is then taken to Sessions Court and most of the time up to High Court, where single-bench judges are busy hearing bail matters only and decide the same in anywhere between 3-4 months to a year. In extreme cases, the matter reaches the Supreme Court.

One arrest leads to spending so much energy and resources of the police, of the judiciary and, of course the general public. The law prescribed and practice of the courts are in contradiction. The situation is no less than a paradox. The amount of money and man-hours wasted is not proportionate to the arrest. A rough estimate of at least 1,000 man-hours per arrest being wasted would not be an exaggeration, in addition to the cost of infrastructure and burden on the nation's resources. Such a situation is irrespective of the rights of the arrested person and without any consideration to the repercussions on the employment, business, reputation, bank strength, loans, and social stigma associated with the arrestee and his family, as well as the repercussions on the mere survival of the family.

5. Analysis of Judicial Trends in Law of Arrest, Custody, Bail and Remand

Pre-Independence

Except for political considerations, the pre-independence period saw arrests being made only on reasonable suspicion or credible information relying upon definite facts and materials. Bails were also granted liberally and refused mostly only when there was cogent ground to apprehend evidence tampering or influencing witnesses. Suited for the Britishers, the gravity of the offence was interpreted to be a relevant factor while declining bail, as done for *Bal Gangadhar Tilak*. Remarkably, the courts had criticized the practice of keeping undertrials in jail, also affirming that courts had unrestricted discretion to grant bail since bail is the rule and jail the exception. However, cancellation of bail was routinely done, often on grounds of the accused being of bad character or for being wealthy or influential. However, on paper, allegations for bail cancellation were interpreted as not vague or of general character.

1950 to Mid-Seventies

Post-independence saw the evolution of law set by the Britishers. Rights of the person being arrested came to be duly recognized by the apex court. These included knowledge about the grounds of arrest, production before a magistrate and the right to legal representation of choice. In the case of *Capt. Jagjit Singh*, the Supreme Court paved the way for future bail jurisprudence while holding that an accused has a right to bail in all bailable offences. Interpreting the parameters for grant of bail in non-bailable offences, the court considered the nature and seriousness of the offence, the character of evidence, circumstances peculiar to the accused, flight risk and a reasonable apprehension of witnesses being tampered with the larger interests of the public as relevant factors for deciding bail. However, the ghosts of preventive detention coming from the British Raj continued till 1977, except for a brief period of two years. There was a new trend of cancelling bail only in cases where any condition is breached or when the accused refused to cooperate with investigation

Post Implementation of the Current-day CrPC

With the introduction of the present day CrPC in 1973, bail jurisprudence saw its golden period, thanks to jurists like Krishna Iyer, J. In the case of *Balchand*, the apex court once again recognized that the basic rule is bail and jail the exception. The very same year, in *Kashmira Singh's* case, the court released the accused on bail even in a murder case, paving the way for release in heinous crimes. The very next year, in the case of *Babu Singh*, the court clarified that a second application for bail with new considerations and changed circumstances is maintainable.

Soon thereafter, a Constitution Bench in the case of *Gurbaksh Singh Sibbia* affirmed that bail is the rule and jail an exception. It further held that no anticipatory bail order be passed in a blanket manner and such bail must also not be denied on mere suspicion of commission of offence. In a pathbreaking pronouncement, the court held that filing of FIR is not a condition precedent to the grant of anticipatory bail and interim bail order can be passed without issuing a notice to the PP. The court propounded the parameters for grant of bail, which continue to hold the field of law till date and primarily include the following:

1. Nature and gravity of the offence.
2. Events leading to the charge.
3. Apprehension of tampering with evidence.
4. Securing the presence of the accused.
5. Balancing individual liberty with public interest.

With these progressive pronouncements, the apex court took upon itself to provide much needed clarity and the high threshold required to cancel a bail through three successive pronouncements, that is, *Gurcharan Singh*, *Sanjay Gandhi* and *Bhagirathsinh*. Around the same time, illegal custody cases came to be heavily criticized by the Supreme Court in the case of *Rudul Shah* wherein the Government was directed to compensate the arrestee. The 1994 judgement in *Joginder Kumar* and the 1997 judgement in *DK Basu* have already been highlighted above and show the resolve of the Supreme Court to prevent arbitrary exercise of powers of arrest.

Recent Trend

Despite the advancement and progress in a bail-centric approach by the apex court, the subsequent pronouncements failed to consider the law laid down in *Sibbia.* It was much later, in 2011, in the case of *Siddharam Satlingappa Mehtre,* the apex court declared these subsequent pronouncements as *per incuriam.* However, till date, the courts continue to be reluctant in granting bail at an early stage, citing the necessity of custodial interrogation as laid in *Anil Sharma's* case, which judgment again fails to consider *Sibbia.* Though *Arnesh Kumar's* case forbids arrest in offences punishable with up to seven years of imprisonment and *Sanjay Chandra's* case further mandates grant of bail post filing of charge sheet if the presence of an accused can be secured during trial, a recent trend of using special statutes, more specifically in economic crimes, to bypass the mandate of the law has been seen wherein arbitrary arrests continue to be made and undertrials continue to languish in jail citing the pendency of further investigation.

The recent trend in special statutes raises an alarming issue of the imposition of additional twin conditions to be satisfied for the grant of bail. Such statutes include the PMLA, the Companies Act, the UAPA, NDPS Act, and the like. These twin conditions mandate that in order to grant bail, the court must be satisfied (1) that there are reasonable grounds for believing that the person is not guilty of the offence and (2) such person is not likely to commit any offence. It is this first condition which is more problematic since it brings in the threshold of charge at the stage of bail. Similarly, once a court has taken cognizance of the offence, satisfying itself about the non-commission of offence becomes a highly unlikely scenario and creates a dichotomy. Even accused persons not arrested during investigation and appearing before court post issuance of summons face the threat of being remanded to custody.

As such, the practical reality today is that jail is the rule and bail the exception. Neither is there any bail jurisprudence being followed, nor is there any uniformity in the grant of bail. Bail orders are not only dependent on the judges, but also on the lawyers and the territorial jurisdiction of the court. While an influential man having the luxury of top lawyers is given a chance to present his case for days at a stretch on priority, a common citizen is given a few minutes to argue his case after months. In my practical experience, there continues to be extremes, both in custody and bail proceedings.

Model Setup

1. No arrest should be made unless and until there is a reasonable satisfaction as to the *bona fides* or genuineness of a complaint as well as the need to effect arrest. Many a time, investigation can be done efficiently by not resorting to arrest and at the same time not infringing upon the accused's fundamental rights. Except in heinous offences, an arrest can be avoided if the investigator issues notice to a person to attend the police station and directs him not to leave the station without permission.
2. The courts must adopt a liberal approach in dealing with bail matters and not be reluctant to rely on the liberty favouring jurisprudence on bail. Any deviation from the mandatory guidelines laid down in the cases of *Joginder Kumar, D.K. Basu and Arnesh Kumar* must be dealt with strictly.
3. The courts must also endeavour to dispose of all bail applications on priority, without exception.
4. At the first production, the magistrate must consider even an oral application opposing remand as a bail application, also using the remand application filed as a response to bail.
5. All courts must give the provisions of bail under the CrPC their true interpretation, restricting themselves to the conditions of bail laid down thereunder, primarily, the triple test, that is, apprehension of tampering with evidence or influencing witnesses or securing the presence of the accused to answer charges.
6. The courts must not be weighed down by uncodified parameters including the nature and gravity of offences and severity of allegations against the accused unnecessarily. They must refrain from entering into the merits of the case and conducting a mini trial at this stage.
7. To curb any mischief, they can take up the cases of bail cancellation in the first instance, should there be any deviation or violation of the bail conditions.
8. The Supreme Court should, as a matter of routine, not be a court hearing bail cases unless a substantial question of law is concerned. Apart from getting more time to be devoted to constitutional mandates, it will help in reducing the pendency of cases.

Trends in Bail, Bail Cancellation and Arrest

I. Pre-independence Period

S.No.	*Case details*	*Relevant points*	*Para.*
		BAIL	
1.	*MaomedYusoof* v. *Emperor* A.I.R. 1926 Rang. 51 Rangoon High Court – Division Bench & *Emperor* v. *Nga San Htwa* A.I.R. 1927 Rang. 205 Rangoon High Court – Full Bench	Mere vague allegations that the prisoner, if released, will tutor witnesses cannot be the only ground for refusal of bail. However, bail can be refused when the prisoner is of such a character that his presence at large will intimidate witnesses, or where there are reasonable grounds for believing that he will use his liberty to suborn evidence.	N/A
2.	*Naranji Premji* v. *Emperor* 1928 SCC OnLine Bom 110 Bombay High Court – Division Bench	If the court is satisfied that there are reasonable grounds for thinking that the applicant is seriously implicated in the charge and that he was one of the assailants, his bail can be refused.	N/A
3.	*Keshav Vasudeo Kortikar v. Emperor* 1933 SCC OnLine Bom 97 Bombay High Court – Division Bench	If a trial is protracted and if accused are not enlarged on bail, they will have undergone an extremely long term of imprisonment, whatever the result of the case may be. Since investigation was complete, there was no danger of tampering with evidence. The status and age of accused afforded guarantee that he will neither abscond nor obstruct prosecution.	N/A
4.	*Surajlal Harilal Majmudar v. Emperor* 1942 SCC OnLine Bom 68 Bombay High Court – Division Bench	The prosecution has a right to oppose bail, and bail can be refused even in bailable offences for cogent reasons. Court has unrestricted discretion to grant bail, wherever the accused might be, whatever be the stage of the proceedings and whatever be the nature of the offence. However, power to grant bail must be judicially exercised, after prosecution is heard.	N/A

S.No.	*Case details*	*Relevant points*	*Para.*
		CANCELLATION OF BAIL	
5.	*Rajah Narendra Lal Khan v. King-Emperor* 1908 SCC OnLine Cal 158 Calcutta High Court – Division Bench	The court cannot, while exercising its discretion for grant of bail, confine its attention only to the question of whether the prisoner is likely to abscond. There may be other circumstances which may affect the question of granting bail to accused who are alleged to have committed crimes of a grave and serious nature.	N/A
6.	*D.R. Guru v. Emperor* 1930 SCC OnLine Bom 126 Bombay High Court – Division Bench	The court considered the following parameters for cancellation of bail: • Wealth and influence of a person, who is likely to win over prosecution witnesses; • Man of bad character or likely to intimidate or otherwise win over the prosecution witnesses. However, allegations for cancelling bail should not be vague or of general character.	N/A
		ARREST	
7.	*Superintendent and Remembrancer of Legal Affairs, Bengal v. Jahir Ali* 1935 SCC OnLine Cal 241 Calcutta High Court – Division Bench	After making an arrest, the police officer is neither bound to release the persons arrested on bail immediately nor inform them that they are entitled to be released on bail.	N/A
8.	*Keshavlal Harilal v. Emperor* 1936 SCC OnLine Bom 31 High Court of Bombay – Division Bench	Arrest is to be made by police officer if thereexists reasonable suspicion or credible information and must be based on definite facts and materials placed, which the officer must consider for himself before he effects arrest in the case.	N/A
		1950-1973	
		BAIL	
1.	*Talab Haji Hussain v. Madhukar Purushottam Mondkar and Ors.* 1958 SCR 1226 Supreme Court of India – 3 Judge Bench	If powers under S.561-A (Now S. 482 CrPC) are exercised by High Court, then bail offered by the accused and accepted by trial court would be cancelled and accused would be ordered to be arrested forthwith. S. 496 (Now S. 436) CrPC does not grant an indefeasible right to be released on bail.	7 & 8

S.No.	*Case details*	*Relevant points*	*Para.*
		If a person accused of a bailable offence is admitted to bail by an order passed by High Court or Court of Sessions, provision of S. 496 (2) becomes applicable and the High Court or Court of Sessions is expressly empowered to cancel bail. This sub-section was added in 1955 by which power the High Court or Court of Sessions was granted the power to cancel bail for persons arrested of non-bailable offences where such persons have been admitted to bail under S.498 (1) (Now S. 439) CrPC.	
2.	*State v. Captain Jagjit Singh* (1962) 3 SCR 622 Supreme Court of India – 3 Judge Bench	The court must first consider whether the offence is bailable or not. If bailable, accused will be granted bail under S. 496 (Now S. 436) CrPC. If non-bailable, further considerations will arise. Considerations which a court must keep in mind are nature and seriousness of offence, character of evidence, circumstances which are peculiar to the accused, a reasonable possibility of the presence of accused not being secured at trial, reasonable apprehension of witnesses being tampered and larger interests of public or state. Further considerations in deciding whether bail should be granted in a non-bailable offence is the nature of the offence and if the offence is of a kind in which bail should not be granted considering its seriousness.	5
3.	*Ratilal Bhanji Mithaini v. Asst. Collector of Customs* (1967) 3 SCR 926 Supreme Court of India – 5 Judge Bench	The court said that if at any subsequent stage post bail is granted under S. 496 (Now S. 436), it is found that any person accused of a bailable offence is intimidating, bribing or tampering with prosecution witness or attempting to abscond, High Court has the power to cause him to be arrested and to commit him to custody. This is an exercise of its inherent powers.	4

S.No.	Case details	Relevant points	Para.
		ARREST	
4.	*State of UP v. Deoman Upadhyaya* (1961) 1 SCR 14 Supreme Court of India – 5 Judge Bench	When a person not in custody approaches a police officer investigating an offence having a bearing of charge which may be made against him, he may appropriately be deemed to have surrendered himself to the police. Procedure does not contemplate any formality before a person is taken into custody. Submission to custody by word or action by a person is sufficient.	12
5.	*State of U.P. v. Abdul Samad* 1962 Supp (3) SCR 915 Supreme Court of India – 3 Judge Bench	When the Constitution makes a provision for production before a magistrate, the requirement is not be treated as any formality but as purposeful and designed to enable the person arrested and detained to be released on bail. In case of lawful deportation, the Magistrate cannot pass an order for release on bail or direct any other custody than that of the officer who has to execute the order of deportation.	12
6.	*State of M.P. v. Shobharam* 1966 2 SCR 239 Supreme Court of India – 3 Judge Bench	Person arrested must be told why he is arrested. Person arrested must not be detained in custody for more than 24 hours without being produced before a Magistrate, unless admitted on bail. Person arrested has a right to consult and to be defended by a lawyer of his choice.	24
		1973-1994	
		BAIL	
1.	*State of Rajasthan v. Balchand* (1977) 4 SCC 308 Supreme Court of India – 2 Judge Bench	The basic rule is bail, not jail, except where there is chance of fleeing, thwarting justice, repeating offences, intimidating witnesses, etc. In most bail cases, not monetary surety but undertaking by relations of the petitioner or organization to which he belongs may be better and more socially relevant.	2, 4

S.No.	Case details	Relevant points	Para.
2.	*Kashmira Singh v. State of Punjab* (1977) 4 SCC 291 Supreme Court of India – 2 Judge Bench	The court considered the issue as to whether it should depart from the practice of not granting bail to accused sentenced to life imprisonment. While releasing the convict on bail, the court highlighted that no practice can be allowed if it causes injustice.	2, 3
3.	*Gurcharan Singh v. State (Delhi Admn.)* (1978) 1 SCC 118 Supreme Court of India – 2 Judge Bench	Sessions Court cannot be oblivious to the mandate of S. 437 CrPC. Intent of S. 437 is to grant bail unless there are exceptional circumstances. Justice to both sides govern the judicious exercise of the court's judicial discretion. Two essentials of bail – (a) likelihood of accused fleeing from justice and (b) witness tampering. Bail cancellation is different from setting aside a bail order. While cancellation generally refers to any violation of bail condition, setting aside the order is done if the bail was granted on wrong parameters.	14, 20, 21, 22, 25 & 29
4.	*Babu Singh v. State of UP* (1978) 1 SCC 579 Supreme Court of India – 2 Judge Bench	Second application for bail with new considerations is maintainable when the first was dismissed. It is rational to do background-check on a man applying for bail. To promote public justice, mechanical detention should be demoted. The law favours granting bail if it is possible.	2, 14, 16, 18, 19 & 23
5.	*State (Delhi Admn.) v. Sanjay Gandhi* (1978) 2 SCC 411 Supreme Court of India – 3 Judge Bench	Just because the prosecution witnesses have turned hostile does not mean that the accused has won them over. Bail cannot be cancelled on this ground. The prosecution need not prove beyond reasonable doubt, proving by test of balance of probabilities is enough for setting aside already granted bail.	13, 14 & 24

S.No.	*Case details*	*Relevant points*	*Para.*
6.	*Gudikanti Narasimhulu v. Public Prosecutor, High Court of A.P.* (1978) 1 SCC 240 Supreme Court of India – Single Judge	The law favours granting bail and the focus is personal freedom. Principles and considerations for granting or refusing bail: • Nature of the charge • Effect on course of justice • Likelihood of witness tampering • Need to deprive personal liberty *Others:* public justice, accused fleeing, etc.	7-12, 16 & 17
7.	*Gurbaksh Singh Sibbia v. State of Punjab* (1980) 2 SCC 565 Supreme Court of India – 5 Judge Bench	Anticipatory bail is, in a sense, an insurance against police custody. Bail is the rule and jail the exception. High/Session Courts can have discretion to grant/deny anticipatory bail because: (a) these are higher experienced courts and (b) every case is unique. Freedom of the individual is as necessary for the survival of society as it is for the egoistic purposes of the individual. Application should not be outrightly rejected just because the punishment is for life or a case for remand of offender to police custody is made out the police. The right to personal freedom cannot be made to depend on compliance to unreasonable restrictions. No presumption can be made that the wealthy will submit themselves to trial and that the poor will run away. Five directions while dealing with an application of anticipatory bail were given. (Para 35 to 39) The order should not be a 'blanket order' exercised in vacuum. The court attempts to balance the individual's right to personal liberty and the investigating rights of the police.	7, 14, 18, 19, 22, 26, 31, 32, 35-39, 41, 42 & 43
8.	*Hussainara Khatoon (IV) v. Home Secy., State of Bihar* (1980) 1 SCC 98 Supreme Court of India – 2 Judge Bench	It is an unjustified deprivation of personal liberty that undertrials who have been in jail longer than maximum term if convicted. Poverty and lack of sureties lead to rejection of bail application of the poor. They must be provided state-appointed lawyers. There is a right to a speedy trial of the accused.	5-10

S.No.	Case details	Relevant points	Para.
9.	*Bhagirathsinh v. State of Gujarat* (1984) 1 SCC 284 Supreme Court of India – 2 Judge Bench	Victim being a political worker is no ground to cancel bail of accused. Trend today is towards granting bail. Power of bail should not be exercised as if the punishment before trial is being imposed.	–
		CANCELLATION OF BAIL	
10.	*Aslam Babalal Desai v. State of Maharashtra* (1992) 4 SCC 363 Supreme Court of India – 3 Judge Bench	The court, interpreting the proviso to S. 167(2) CrPC, observed that while the accused was entitled to bail by default and not on merits in case the investigating officer did not complete the investigation and file the charge sheet within the prescribed period. In the event the prosecution sought cancellation of bail, such bail cannot be cancelled simply because a charge sheet was subsequently filed.	39, 40
		ARREST	
11.	*Kanu Sanyal v. Distt. Magistrate* (1973) 2 SCC 674 Supreme Court of India – 5 Judge Bench	While dealing with an application for a writ of habeas corpus under Article 32, the court may not require the body of the person detained to be brought before the court. It is an idle formality. Instead, the focus should be on examining the validity of detention.	7
12.	*Rudul Sah v. State of Bihar* (1983) 4 SCC 141 Supreme Court of India – 2 Judge Bench	The petitioner was detained illegally for over 14 years after acquittal. The govt. was directed to release such illegally detained people and pay adequate compensation for their rehabilitation.	7, 9
13.	*Joginder Kumar v. State of U.P.* AIR 1994 SC 1349 Supreme Court of India – 2 Judge Bench	The court held that although the police had discretionary powers to arrest a person in a cognizable case, every arrest had to be justified. Arrests could not be made in a routine manner. Every arrest should be made after the police officer reached a reasonable satisfaction after some investigation that the complaint was genuine and bona fide, the accused was complicit, and the arrest was necessary and justified.	20

1995 – Present			
BAIL			
S.No.	*Case Details*	*Relevant Points*	*Para.*
1.	*Salauddin Abdulsamad Shaikh v. State of Maharashtra* 3 1996 SCC (1) 667 Supreme Court of India – 3 Judge Bench	The court held that anticipatory bail is granted in anticipation of arrest in non-bailable cases, but that does not mean that the regular court, which is to try the offender, is sought to be by-passed and that is the reason why the High Court very rightly fixed the outer date for the continuance of the bail and on the date of its expiry directed the petitioner to move the regular court for bail. That is the correct procedure to follow because it must be realized that when the Court of Session or the High Court is granting anticipatory bail, it is granted at a stage when the investigation is incomplete and, therefore, it is not informed about the nature of evidence against the alleged offender.	2, 3
2.	*State (CBI) v. Anil Sharma* (1997) 7 SCC 187 Supreme Court of India – 3 Judge Bench	Anticipatory bail was refused on the ground that in cases of corruption in high places where accused has held high offices, he may wield wide influence and the investigation could suffer. The court observed as follows: "In a case like this effective interrogation of suspected person is of tremendous advantage in disinterring many useful information and also materials which would have been concealed Succession of such interrogation would elude if the suspected person knows that he is well protected and insulted by a pre-arrest bail during the time he interrogated".	4, 6
3.	*Prahlad Singh Bhati v. NCT Delhi & Ors.* (2001) 4 SCC 280 Supreme Court of India – 2 Judge Bench	The court mentioned that relevant grounds which play a vital role in deciding the bail application are the possibility for repetition of crime, the time lag between the date of occurrence and the conclusion of the trial, illegal detention, and undue delay in the trial of the case.	8

S.No.	*Case details*	*Relevant points*	*Para.*
4.	*Ram Govind Upadhyay v. Sudarshan Singh & Ors.* (2002) 3 SCC 598 Supreme Court of India – 2 Judge Bench	The court held certain circumstances need to be considered while granting bail, including where the applicant has already been in custody, and the trial is not likely to conclude for some time, which can be characterized as unreasonable.	4, 8 & 9
5.	*State of Maharashtra v. Sitaram Popat Vital* (2004) 7 SCC 521 Supreme Court of India – 2 Judge Bench	Few factors to consider while granting bail are: • Nature of accusation, severity of punishment and nature of supporting evidence; • Reasonable apprehension of tampering of the witness or apprehension of threat to complainant; *Prima facie* satisfaction of the court in support of the charge.	6
6.	*Satish Jaggi v. State of Chattisgarh & Ors.* 2007 ALL SCR 1438 Supreme Court of India – 2 Judge Bench	At the stage of bail, the court can only go into the question of a prima facie case being established. It cannot go into the credibility and reliability of witnesses put up by the prosecution, which can only be tested during trial.	5, 12
7.	*Sumit v. State of U.P.* 2010 Cri.L.J. 1435 (SC) Supreme Court of India – Single Judge	It was held that even if there are other criminal cases pending, accused should be granted bail.	N/A
8.	*Siddharam Satlingappa Mehtre v. State of Maharashtra & Ors* (2011) 1 SCC 694 Supreme Court of India – 2 Judge Bench	It is important to maintain a balance between personal liberty and social interest. The duration of the anticipatory bail cannot be limited by time because there is no limitation set by any law. Therefore, wide discretion has been conferred to court to grant anticipatory bail.	84, 123 & 126
9.	*Sanjay Chandra v. CBI* (2012) 1 SCC 40 Supreme Court of India – 2 Judge Bench	Gravity of the crime alone cannot be a decisive ground to deny bail. Post filing of charge sheet, bail should be granted to accused. The purpose is to secure the presence of accused to answer charges.	39, 40

S.No.	*Case details*	*Relevant points*	*Para.*
10.	*Bhadresh Seth v. State of Gujarat* (2016) 1 SCC 152 Supreme Court of India – Single Judge	The court granted bail to the appellant noting that there is no possibility of his fleeing from justice and appellant has participated in proceedings during period of investigation. The Bench further noted that as observed by the Constitution Bench of this Court in Sibbia, S. 438 CrPC calls for a liberal interpretation as it is conceptualized in Article 21.	21, 26
11.	*Rukmani Mahato v. State of Jharkhand* (2017) 15 SCC 574 Supreme Court of India – 2 Judge Bench	When the Supreme Court or a High Court or even a Sessions Judge grants interim anticipatory bail and the matter is pending before that court, there can be no occasion for the accused to appear and surrender before the learned trial court and seek regular bail. Surrender and a bail application in such circumstances is nothing but an abuse of the process of law.	9
12.	*P. Chidambaram v. Directorate of Enforcement* (2019) 9 SCC 63 Supreme Court of India – 3 Judge Bench	Availability for further investigation and interrogation, no apprehension of evading the process of law and no possibility of tampering with the evidence or influencing the witnesses are enough to grant bail.	N/A
13.	*Sushila Aggarwal & Ors. v. State (NCT of Delhi) & Ors.* 2020 SCC OnLine SC 98 Supreme Court of India – 5 Judge Bench	Protection under S. 438 CrPC cannot be invariably limited to a fixed time. However, depending on the facts of the case, the courts may impose certain conditions and time limit. Additionally, the protection provided by an anticipatory bail does not end when the accused is summoned, or charges are framed. It can be continued until the trial ends. However, if the circumstances of the case require a fixed time limit or imposition of certain conditions, then, the court can impose the same.	84
14.	*Satender Kumar Antil v. CBI* (2021) 10 SCC 773 Supreme Court of India – 2 Judge Bench	Offences were categorized and guidelines laid down for grant of bail post filing of charge sheet. The endeavour was to promote bail, depending on the facts of the case.	3-7

CANCELLATION OF BAIL

S.No.	*Case details*	*Relevant points*	*Para.*
15.	*Puran & Ors. v. Rambilas & Ors.* (2001) 6 SCC 338 Supreme Court of India – Single Judge	Bail can be cancelled even when there is no evidence that the conditions of bail are being infringed. One ground for the same is where a 'perverse order' granting bail is passed in a heinous crime, ignoring the material and evidence on the record, and, or without giving reasons. Interests of justice require that such arbitrary exercise of discretion be corrected.	10
16.	*Kalyan Chandra Sarkar v. Rajesh Ranjan & Ors.* (2004) 7 SCC 528 Supreme Court of India – 3 Judge Bench	Although an accused has a right to make successive applications for grant of bail, the court entertaining such subsequent bail applications has a duty to consider the reasons and grounds on which the earlier bail applications were rejected. The court also has a duty to record what are the fresh grounds which persuaded it to take a view different from the one taken in the earlier applications. In this case, since no fresh ground was recorded by the High Court while granting bail, bail was cancelled.	20
17.	*Dinesh M. N. (S.P.) v. State of Gujarat* (2008) 5 SCC 66 Supreme Court of India – 3 Judge Bench	Even though the CrPC does not intend for the court granting bail to re-appreciate the evidence on record, the court dealing with an application for the cancellation of bail pursuant to S. 439(2) can take into account whether irrelevant materials were also considered. Once it is concluded that bail was granted on untenable grounds, the plea of absence of supervening circumstances has no leg to stand.	23, 26
18.	*CBI v. Vijay Sai Reddy* (2013) 7 SCC 452 Supreme Court of India – 2 Judge Bench	The cancellation of bail entails undertaking a review of a decision already made by a court, and it should be exercised 'very sparingly' by any court of law.	36
19.	*Abdul Basit @ Raju & Ors. etc. v. Md. Abdul Kadir Choudhary* (2014) 10 SCC 754 Supreme Court of India – 2 Judge Bench	As no expression provision for reviewing an order granting bail exists under the Criminal Procedure Code, the High Court becomes functus officio and S. 362 CrPC applies, barring the review of the order of the High Court granting bail to	26

S.No.	Case details	Relevant points	Para.
		the petitioner-accused. Even though the cancellation of bail rides on the satisfaction and discretion of the court under S. 439(2) CrPC, it does not vest the power of review in the court which granted bail. Even in the light of fact of misrepresentation by the accused during the grant of bail, the High Court could not have entertained the prayer by sitting in review of its judgment.	
		ARREST	
20.	*Citizens of Democracy v. State of Assam & Ors.* (1995) 3 SCC 743 Supreme Court of India – 2 Judge Bench	Handcuffing cannot be forced on an undertrial prisoner in absence of a well-grounded basis that must be recorded. Any violation would attract the penal provisions of the Contempt of Courts Act.	16, 17 & 21
21.	*D.K. Basu v. State of West Bengal* AIR 1997 SC 610 Supreme Court of India – 2 Judge Bench	While examining the issue of increasing number of custodial deaths in India, a total of 11 binding guidelines were issued. The court mandated the preparation of a memo at the time of arrest; identification tags for policemen; an entry in the police diary disclosing details of arrest; conspicuous display of notice of arrest on the notice board; sending copies of all documents to the area magistrate and entitling the arrestee with the right to medical examination at the time of arrest; inform one friend or relative of the arrest as soon as practicable. Failure to comply with these requirements shall render the concerned official liable for departmental action and contempt of court proceedings. 35, 36	
22.	*State of Maharashtra v. Christian Community Welfare Council of India* (2003) 8 SCC 546 Supreme Court of India – 2 Judge Bench	A lady can be arrested by a male police officer in the absence of a female constable at any time of the day, for reasons to be recorded in writing either before or immediately after arrest if it is not possible to have a lady constable present and/or if ensuring her presence would impede the investigation.	9

S.No.	*Case details*	*Relevant points*	*Para.*
23.	*Arnesh Kumar v. State of Bihar* (2014) 8 SCC 273 Supreme Court of India – 2 Judge Bench	Arrests curtail freedom and cause humiliation and therefore, cannot be made unscrupulously without following protocol. S. 41 CrPC lays down pre-conditions for arrest and S. 41A provides for accused not to be arrested if they comply with the notice issued by the police officer (unless there is reason for arrest, after complying with S. 41 requirements that the police officer must record). These provisions need to be adhered to strictly to ensure that police officers do not make arrests unnecessarily and Magistrates do not authorise detention casually and mechanically.	6, 9 & 11
24.	*Siddharth v. State of UP* (2022) 1 SCC 676 Supreme Court of India – 2 Judge Bench	Distinction between existence of power to arrest and justification for exercise of such power. Simply because charge sheet is filed cannot mandate arrest of an accused who has cooperated with investigation.	6-12

6. Search and Seizure

Powers of search and seizure are part and parcel of an investigation. Such powers serve a multi-fold purpose. They ensure the production or safe custody of books, papers, digital data or other evidence. In cases of documentary evidence or for offences involving recovery, they are an important step to prove the case by securing the evidence and/or the case property. Additionally, they act as a retributive mechanism and facilitate in securing the value of the property under question, which is suspected to be derived from the commission of the offence and which may otherwise be alienated. The seized property can be forfeited as per law after conviction.

The broad parameters pertaining to search and seizure have been defined in the CrPC. In cases of search, the police may choose to do so with or without obtaining warrants from court. All such proceedings must be in the presence of at least two independent witnesses who are reliable and respectable inhabitants of the locality, and if no such witness is available, the witnesses can be from other localities or formal witnesses.

The police are well within its right to use any or such force, as necessary, to progress with the proceedings. The powers of seizure can only be exercised in cases of moveable property. Although S. 102 CrPC speaks of seizure, since certain properties such as bank accounts, shares in dematerialized form, and the like are incapable of being seized, freezing has been read into seizure. The seizure must be reported to a magistrate forthwith and the property is generally produced before the court. In such cases, the magistrate may choose to impound the property.

In the Indian context, the law mandates that a mere violation of a provision pertaining to search does not vitiate the prosecution case unless the accused was prejudiced. Such violation is a mere irregularity.

Practical Application

A layman would find the powers of search and seizure to be draconian. However, these powers have been given to the police for critical purposes, mentioned above. It is the implementation of these powers which remains questionable.

The instances of unnecessary raids and indiscriminate seizures without any application of mind remain an area of concern. The vast majority of search and seizure proceedings serve no purpose.

While a confession in police custody is inadmissible, the recovery of items based on such confession is admissible. Many a time, the entire operation is a farce with the proceedings taking place only on paper. There have been instances of the police itself planting incriminating material and then seizing the same to prove their case, also taking the help of the complainant to plant the articles.

A Contrast to the American Criminal Justice System

The courts in the USA are strict in granting permission to conduct a search. The prosecution must specify the particulars of the search, including the place, property, time, mode and manner before the court. Such application must disclose the source and the reliability of the information and the reasons to believe such information. The courts will then apply their mind to the facts. The whole proceeding shall stand vitiated if it is later found that the application of mind by the court was improper.

Unlike India, the USA follows the principle of 'fruits of a poisonous tree'. Anything seized or proceeded with pursuant to an illegal search is also illegal. The search has to be for a specific thing in a specific offence. Any other incriminating material not mentioned in the search warrant, despite revealing some serious crime, is inadmissible, but for exceptions which are strict and few.

The proceedings in the USA primarily revolve around probable cause. Even the automobile exception under which officers are allowed to search the vehicle as well as any container or boot, not in normal sight, is based on probable cause. In the absence of any such cause, the action is invalid since searches otherwise must be *'in plain view'*. A few other exceptions to the normal rule include the Special Needs Doctrine pertaining to border actions, national security, school searches and the like. Such restrictions also stand waived in case of consent searches.

If we closely scrutinize the above procedure as is practised in the USA, two things are evident, (1) independent witnesses are not necessary, and

(2) there is a huge onus on the capability and integrity of both the police and the judiciary. This is in stark contrast to India where it is necessary to have a reliable and independent witness. It means that the police are as such not believed to be fair. Additionally, the onus on the prosecution is much more in the USA since any irregularity is enough to vitiate the entire case.

Need of the Hour

It is not necessary to change our laws. What is required is deterrence, both in the police and the judiciary. If there is no deterrence, we will continue to have partial search and seizures. As a first step to curb this menace, the magistrate, while issuing warrants, must apply his mind to determine whether the same is necessary since issuance of a search warrant is a serious matter.

While adjudicating a case, the, magistrate must examine whether there is a genuine recovery or a forced recovery. The conduct of the investigating officer should be impeccable, and any recovery must be proved beyond reasonable doubt. The court must not take the prosecution version as the gospel truth and refrain from simply relying on the evidence collected during such proceedings. No doubt, such recoveries have a probative value but that alone cannot be the basis of a conviction.

There must also be an effort to see whether the requirement of witnesses from the local area has not been followed only to suit the prosecution case. The search officer must be put to prove his case about the absence or refusal of the witnesses in the locality and the action he took against these persons for such disobedience. A model search and seizure form, to address these concerns, is given below.

Search and Seizure Form

FIR No: .... U/s: ....

Reference No: ....

1. Nature of Property Seized/Recovered:
2. Date of Seizure/Recovery:
3. Place of Seizure/Recovery, with description:
4. Details of person from whom seized/recovered:
    a. Name: ....
    b. Father's/Husband's Name: ....
    c. Sex: ....
    d. Age: ....
    e. Address: ....
5. **Identification required:** Yes/No
6. **Details of properties seized/recovered:**

S. No.	*Description*	*Volume*

7. The said properties were seized in accordance with law & in presence of witnesses:

Particulars	*Witness 1*	*Witness 2*
Name		
Father's/Husband's Name		
Sex		
Age		
Address		

[In case the witnesses are not from the same locality, then the following:]

a. Names of Persons asked to become witnesses:

b. Addresses of Persons asked to become witnesses:

c. Whether any action taken against such refusal, and if so, what action:

8. Action taken/recommended for disposal of perishable property (if required):

9. Action taken/recommended for keeping of valuable property (if required):

Acknowledgment

Name: ....

Address: ....

Signature: ....

Witness 1 **Witness 2**

....

(Signature) *(Signature)*

(Signature and Stamp of the Search Officer)

7. Attachment and Confiscation

Attachment

Attachment and seizure reduce the risk of alienation and disposal of property. The police, as compared to the Enforcement Directorate, have restricted powers of attachment. While the CrPC has adequate provisions relating to seizure of a property, attachment of property is governed in terms of the Criminal Law Ordinance, 1944. The power, though rarely exercised, helps the police in securing the value of the property, while also not denying the benefits of enjoyment to such person in whose possession the property remains. The attachment however is on the orders of the District Judge of the area on an application made in this behalf by a sanctioning authority in the concerned government. It is for the same reason that these powers are not usually exercised by the police.

Confiscation

The court has the power to confiscate whatever is seized and attached. Confiscation is a serious step and cannot take place without the permission of the court unlike seizure and attachment, which is done by the police and investigating authorities.

While the objective is clear, there is a need to revisit the scheme of confiscation post-trial to address the issue of protracted attachment. Property such as shares in a company are often viable and once attached may tend to be in excess of the amount attached. Similarly, their value may completely plunge and render the option of recovering proceeds of crime as futile. Another example is of wild or exotic animals that are kept attached for long periods which are not only inhuman but extremely illogical. Similar is the situation with drugs. Their attachment causes custody issues. Since they are illegal substances which cannot be returned, they should be destroyed as early as possible to reduce the risk of their illegal smuggling from *malkhanas* and subsequent trade and distribution. Though the apex court has already crystallized the law on continuous retention of property, in turn favouring its release on certain conditions, the reality at the ground level continues to differ.

8. Forensic and Medical Investigation

History

Evidence collection is the bedrock of a good and competent investigation. Within evidence collection, forensic evidence assumes a crucial role. It helps apply medical knowledge and science to the purpose of the law and to meet the ends of justice. In fact, forensic evidence is essential for scientific investigation, and in the absence of it, it is often difficult to ascertain how the crime actually took place. The Supreme Court has on several occasions reiterated the importance of scientific investigation in criminal cases. Simply put, a scientific investigation is an investigation mechanism which relies upon scientific instruments to assess the veracity and authenticity of evidence collected when a crime takes place.

In ancient India, the major medico-legal treatise was Kautilya's *Arthashashtra*, which stated that death (homicide) could be caused by: (1) stopping the breathing (strangling/hanging/asphyxiation/drowning); (2) physical injury (beating/throwing from a height); (3) poisoning (poisons/snake or insect bite/narcotic drugs). The *Arthashastra* endeavoured to provide a kind of forensic evidence, as envisaged today, in a very basic but progressive manner in those times.

Present-day Tools

The success of criminal investigations was mostly dependent on forced confessions of the accused and, or testimonies of witnesses and continued till the pre-independence era. In fact, it was only in 1858 that the use of fingerprinting in criminal investigations was introduced in India. In the absence of adequate forensic tools, it was difficult to accurately discern the exact nature of the injury sustained by the victim and was also responsible for misplaced adjudication of cases.

Post-independence, with the establishment of colleges and universities focussing on forensic medicine and toxicology, there has been a movement towards using scientific and forensic tools to conduct criminal investigations. In fact, in recent times, the advancement in technology and science has substantially aided enforcement agencies in this regard. An example of this is the use of advanced DNA tools for the testing and analysis of blood and hair samples of both the victim and the accused. In cases of homicide and rape, this DNA analysis is essential in incriminating the accused. Further, other medical tests also help examine the exact gravity and nature of the injury sustained. In fact, a thorough examination of the injury is also important in understanding the kind of weapon used by the accused to commit the crime. The nature and depth of the wound allows the medical examiner to often offer conclusive evidence of the weapon. In cases of homicide, the emergence of new tools in post-mortem or autopsy examination have helped investigative agencies to ascertain the time of the death, cause of death and any other factor surrounding the death, which may have been missed during a prior cursory examination of the body. The examination is not limited to the body of the victim or the accused. It extends to the forensic examination of the clothes worn, shoes, undergarments (of particular relevance in rape or assault cases), any other accessory or object carried, including jewellery, bag, wallet, of both the victim and the accused.

Apart from examining the injury, scientific tools also assist investigative agencies in determining the time of the incident and the location of both the victim and the accused. A simple example of this is a mobile phone. With the rampant use of mobile phones in India, enforcement and investigative agencies are now able to trace and track the time and location of people involved in the crime and resultantly are able to thread together the chain of events with accuracy. This is useful because time is of essence in criminal investigation to ensure that evidence is collected promptly. In addition to mobile phones, CCTV cameras have also assumed significant importance in investigations. Forensic examination also extends to the crime scene and all case property seized. DNA fingerprinting involves examination of all objects seized during the investigation. Further, forensic tools such as narco-analysis and polygraph tests are also used to check the veracity of the accused or witnesses' statements, which however is subject to the consent of the person. It may be important to mention that even if such evidence has admissibility issues, it is a critical tool in furtherance of investigation.

Need of the Hour

After an investigation is concluded, the police file a charge sheet which often includes a detailed report sent by the FSL. The charge sheet is then submitted to the court. During court proceedings, the FSL report is perused by the judges. Where there is cogent forensic evidence on record, either proving or disproving the role of the accused, courts generally rely on the forensic evidence to determine the guilt of the accused. In some recent cases, the Supreme Court has held that the question of whether a specific offence has been committed or not should be a legal conclusion and not a conclusion solely dictated by forensic evidence. This is problematic since the loopholes and technicalities in law help in shielding the accused despite clinching scientific evidence on record. Courts must rely on such genuine evidence to determine the guilt of the accused. However, in cases where there is no credible forensic evidence available, legal conclusions should take precedence. Further, in cases where forensic evidence is not available due to a lapse by the police, there should be adverse inference drawn in favour of the accused, also taking action against the erring official.

We are in an era of science and technology. The rampant growth in medicine, science and artificial intelligence has now enabled investigative agencies to simulate the entire crime scene. The role played by forensics in investigation is important. It is critical for investigative agencies to fully utilize the potential of forensic investigation and get better results. Scientific investigation is both a boon as well as a bane. While it can be used to prove a case by telephone records, location mapping, etc., at the same time it can prove challenging to belie the fairness of investigation.

As a footnote, I may mention that in my experience, in most parts of the country, the use of scientific evidence is well received when it is against the accused. However, in most cases where it favours the accused or the defence presents sufficient doubt about the investigation, either questioning the forensic evidence collected by the police or where the cross-examination dents the authenticity of the forensic evidence, such doubt is not as well received by the courts. The purpose of forensic investigation and use of scientific evidence is defeated.

III

PRE-TRIAL PROCEEDINGS

1. Notice under S. 91 CrPC

Although S. 91 CrPC is an important power with the police in aid of an investigation, it is also a power which can be exercised by the court at any stage and, as such, is being dealt in the pre-trial proceedings. While the present discussion will briefly summarize the advantages of the section before proceeding to the stage of inquiry, its import post investigation has been dealt with in subsequent chapters.

As mentioned already in an earlier chapter, S. 91 CrPC deals with the production of documents or other things through a notice. Such notice can be given directly by the police officer or an application can be moved before the court, so as to compel any person to produce the documents asked for in the notice. It is really necessary to understand the import of the section, which continues to be an understated and underused provision as a tool of investigation.

During the normal course of investigation, the investigator, instead of asking for documents, issues a notice under S. 160 CrPC. The result is that the person to whom notice has been sent to join investigation is unclear as to why he has been summoned. On the contrary, if a notice under S. 91 CrPC is given, essentially what is required to be given are only the documents and nothing else. On submission of documents, the requirements of the notice are met and the person would be more comfortable to assist in the investigation.

On receipt of the documents, the investigator should, in the first instance, consider the documents. Only when any explanation is needed with regard to the documents or the source needs to be identified or the authenticity is an issue should notice under S. 160 CrPC be given. Such notice under S. 160 CrPC should mention the reason for summoning the person to appear in person. This would enable the person to whom summons have been issued to come prepared to answer questions put to him.

Practical Application

It is necessary to elaborate on the scheme that should be adopted rather than the one that is practised. In brief, the investigators keep the people who are worthy witnesses, who not only assist the investigation but are key to the success of the case, under fear and uncertainty. Further, they are also treated in a manner which sometimes is harsher than that of the accused. In today's context, without any rhyme or reason, we make a large number of witnesses vulnerable. Such witnesses go to lawyers, spend money, get tutored and in such cases, the investigation is hampered. Moreover, applications are made in courts in many cases where the lawyers are either not well versed in law, more so in smaller towns, or when the lawyers do not give the best suited advice to the client. The time of the court and that of the investigating agencies, the PP, the court staff and the use of infrastructure is an additional burden on the country, in addition to the loss of manhours.

Need of the Hour

In the proposed scheme, it is suggested that witnesses or anybody who is being investigated should be given dignity and respect as is encompassed under Article 21 of the Constitution of India. The investigators instead of making a roving inquiry or groping in the dark should seek as many documents as possible through the use of S. 91 CrPC. If such notice is not adhered to, the court is there to compel any such person to produce documents. In any case, where the person is being evasive or not cooperative, such conduct should be noted in the DDR and should also be brought to the attention of the court while moving an application under S. 91 CrPC.

Once the documents are produced, the same should be evaluated and the next course of action should be discussed in-house. Such course should be then given effect to. It may include recording the satisfaction vis-à-vis such witness, who should then be called if there are any documents which have to be made a part of the charge sheet and his statement under S. 161 CrPC should be recorded. There can also be a further course of seeking more documents based on the evaluation of the documents produced earlier. Alternatively, there can also be a situation where the explanation of the person with regard to the document so produced is necessary. In such a case, notice under S. 160 CrPC should be issued and it should in brief detail the reasons for summoning such person so that the meeting which he is supposed to do with the investigator is effective and fruitful.

This process will not only give respect and dignity to the witness but also save everyone's time and energy. It will also be more effective and help the investigation and the investigating agencies to reach a conclusion with minimum court interference and, or distortions made by consultation of legal experts.

Such a recourse is specific to cases of documentary evidence, especially white-collar crimes, cheating, forgery, cases investigated by central agencies. In cases of special crimes or violent crimes, this recourse may not be followed in such meticulous detail.

2. Charge Sheet

Upon the completion of investigation, the investigator files a Police Report (referred to as Charge sheet), which will contain the names of parties, the nature of information, the list of witnesses and documents being relied upon by the prosecution for its case, the offence committed (if any) and the accused, details of arrest and custody (if any) and such other details. Any report without these basic essentials would not qualify as a complete report, and would rather be called an incomplete charge sheet, entitling the accused to default bail for failure to complete investigation within the mandated timeline.

Supplementary Charge Sheet

The final report may be supplemented by a Supplementary Report (charge sheet) which is generally when the investigator obtains further oral or documentary evidence. Such report is a continuation of the previous report and is filed when certain aspects of investigation have been delayed for various reasons including abscondence of the accused, absence of records, fresh discoveries, etc. Such report is a result of further investigation, which can be both at the directions of the court or at the behest of the police itself.

Unrelied Records

Unlike in the USA and the United Kingdom, where the jurisprudence has evolved and mandates that the prosecution must not only disclose but also provide for all evidence in favour of the accused, Indian law does not mandate such disclosures. It was only very recently in 2021 that the Supreme Court directed that the prosecution must file a list of documents, statements, objects and exhibits that are not relied upon by the investigator. The apex court mandated providing only a list of the same to the accused since such records are a part of the investigation and need not be submitted in court or be subjected to any investigation. The disclosure, as directed, is enough to ensure a free and fair trial since the accused through an application and even the judge on his own can exercise powers for summoning such records under S. 91 CrPC, if it is shown that they are crucial to the defence of the accused, depending on the facts and circumstances of each case. Even at the stage of compliances under S. 207 or S. 208 CrPC, if something does not form a part of the charge sheet but is relevant evidence that should have been collected by the police, the accused can make such an application. The application may lead to further investigation by police. The court can even ask for records to be made part of the judicial record if it is shown that the record is of stellar quality and unimpeachable with respect to its source and authenticity, for example, bank statements, government data and the like. The rationale behind the same is to give a fair chance to the accused for his defence, also empowering the court at the time of framing of charge to do justice.

Proposed Steps

To effectively address concerns regarding the fairness of the investigation and to stall any effort to delay the inquiry or trial, there should be a column in the challan that the accused was asked if he voluntarily wants to rely on any material and he had undertaken that he does not want to do so.

Before the commencement of the trial, there should be a conclusive undertaking by the investigator that the investigation is complete and the trial be progressed. The investigator, while finalizing the charge sheet, must refrain from bringing repetitive or unnecessary witnesses. The investigator must also effectively use column 2 of the charge sheet, naming the persons against whom no case has been found or who have not been chargesheeted for lack of evidence or such other reasons, which reasons must also form a part of the charge sheet.

While recording the statements of witnesses under S. 161 CrPC, the investigators must desist from using their own language unless dealing with such witnesses who are low on their intelligent quotient or are unable to explain themselves. In such cases, the investigator must understand the statement and write a coherent account, duly mentioning the same in the statement so recorded. This will help the prosecution in projecting that the witness is likely to falter in cross-examination. The cross-examination of such witnesses should be actively supervised by the judge, who shall take precautions in explaining questions more clearly to ensure fairness of justice.

3. Cognizance

Departure from the Old CrPC

S. 190 CrPC deals with cognizance. Under CrPC, 1898, cognizance was taken of the accused. However, this was changed under the new CrPC wherein now the cognizance is taken of the offence and not of the accused.

This change brought about a very important shift because earlier the court had to apply its mind each time a new accused was added in the case. It was a cumbersome procedure to take cognizance because every time the role of the offender and the *prima facie* guilt of the offender was necessary to be arrived at before taking cognizance. Now, once cognizance of the offence is taken, it is easier and practical to add an accused.

Meaning of the term 'Cognizance'

The jurisprudence on the issue is well settled. Cognizance is not one of the topics of criminal jurisprudence where there is a scope for much debate. The law as has been laid out is succinct and involves the following prerequisites to conclude taking cognizance, which means as under:

1. The Magistrate/Judge has applied his judicious mind in the criminal proceeding; or
2. The Magistrate/Judge has acted upon such judicial application of mind; or
3. The Judge has taken judicial notice of the offence.

Need of the Hour

It is important to note that taking cognizance should be by a reasoned order which should indicate an application of mind. Courts have time and again criticized the cryptic orders of cognizance which at times are as short as '*Report filed and perused. Issue summons to accused*'. Even though this order is complete in the larger sense of showing application of mind but in essence, if the report is filed at the same time, it is questionable and rather impossible for the judge to get time to read the entire report and arrive at a conclusion while dealing with the entire list of details. However, such orders continue to be passed in a routine manner. Therefore, it is proposed as under:

1. While the Police Report is being filed in court, the PP should in brief explain to the judge about the nature of investigation, *prima facie* proof of allegations against each accused or of the offence, based on the documents that have been filed with the report.
2. The entire procedure for *prima facie* conclusions usually would not exceed 10 minutes and therefore, even though an elaborate order is not required, the court would be in a position to record its satisfaction after a perusal of the record and after hearing arguments on cognizance. This alone would be sufficient even though it does not mention the reasons to pass an order taking cognizance. An ideal scenario however would be if the judge mentions a paragraph for the reasons of recording his satisfaction for taking cognizance.
3. The Supreme Court had way back in 1990 indicated that the exercise of taking cognizance should not be a mere formality. The onus to discharge such functions is very high on the magistrate since he has three options at the time of taking cognizance: one is to take cognizance, second is to reject findings and discharge all the accused from the case and third is to record his dissatisfaction with the investigation and ask the investigator to do further investigation. Therefore, cognizance should be taken by actual application of mind in a judicious manner by the court and not mechanically.

4. Stage of Compliance under S. 207 CrPC

All documents and statements which the prosecution proposes to rely upon after investigation and which have been forwarded to the magistrate are required to be provided to the accused under S. 207 CrPC. This section gives the accused access to the evidence collected by investigating agencies, which will be used during trial. Not only is this exercise an important stepping-stone for building the defence of the accused, but it also upholds the right of an accused to a free and fair trial.

S. 207 CrPC casts a duty upon the court to supply all documents and statements or their parts that they have chosen to use to establish their case, i.e., relied upon documents. This includes giving documents which are legible and, or translated versions. Until such stage is complete, the court does not move ahead with the trial or commit the case for trial in appropriate cases. These documents can be used by the accused at the stage of framing of charge to show how no case is made out to proceed with the trial. The documents can also be used to point out loopholes in the investigation.

The stage contemplated under S. 207 CrPC is narrow and concerns only provision of documents. The court cannot study the evidentiary value of the documents relied upon by the prosecution at this stage and must restrict its supervisory powers to the extent of provision of all documents annexed with the charge sheet. The role of the court is more or less administrative in nature at this stage.

The accused usually requests for certain documents which have not been relied upon by the prosecution. These may include such documents which had been previously supplied by the accused to the investigating agency during investigation and may be important for the accused to establish his innocence.

Brady's Principle and Position in India

This issue whether it is mandatory for the court to provide documents not relied upon by it has caught the attention of several high courts and the apex court. The principle, famously known as 'Brady's principle' in

American law, stipulates that suppression of either inculpatory and exculpatory evidence by the PP violates due process and rights of the accused. Such violation could also lead to a mistrial.

While Indian law does not prescribe to such principle, the apex court in its recent decision in *In Re: To issue certain guidelines regarding inadequacies and deficiencies in criminal trials (Suo Moto Writ (Crl.) No. (S) 1/2017* has attempted to amalgamate American law with the legal principles of India, to widen the scope of S. 207 CrPC and resolve this contentious issue regarding unrelied documents. Without touching upon the mandatory requirement of providing unrelied documents, the apex court has with the intention of providing absolute disclosure and ample opportunity to the accused to defend himself, directed the prosecution to provide a list of all unrelied documents, statements, and exhibits to the accused. These documents, often lying in the *malkhanas* of the investigating agency, may be inspected by the accused in as far as the recent judicial trends can be interpreted. The accused can later, at the stage of charge, prove how and why these documents are of stellar quality and must be admitted as evidence. However, the law in this regard is still evolving and is under scrutiny of courts.

Role of the PP

While there are adequate safeguards in place in the system to ensure that during trial, documents sought to be brought on record by the accused are discovered and considered by the courts, the role of the PP needs to be minutely examined. It is the primary duty of the PP to discover the truth and his objective is not constrained to finding of guilt. Thus, in case the PP is in possession of any document which is proof of the innocence of the accused and yet chooses to conceal the same, the same amounts to gross misconduct and appropriate proceedings should be initiated against the PP. Since the role of the PP includes ensuring that the accused is treated fairly, it is but obvious that the exercise of providing documents must be undertaken in good faith and belief. However, in circumstances where the PP has also been kept in the dark by the police and such fact becomes known, then necessary action must also be initiated against the investigator.

5. Committal of Cases

In all cases triable exclusively by a Sessions Court, the magistrate commits the case to the concerned Sessions Court once the necessary compliances of supply of documents have been made. The powers of committal are more administrative in nature than judicial. The magistrate acts as a post office and plays a passive role, since the magistrate has no jurisdiction to try these cases.

While the apex court has had divergent views on the scope and extent of powers under S. 193 CrPC which talks about 'Cognizance by Court of Sessions', the controversy was settled by a constitutional bench in *Dharampal's* case. However, the court, while agreeing with the principles laid down previously in the case of *Kishun Singh*, restricted the exercise of such powers to only summoning additional accused. Under the law laid down by the apex court, if the Sessions Court is of the opinion that apart from the persons charge sheeted by the police, there are others involved in the commission of offences, it must proceed against such persons and summon them under S. 193 CrPC. The Sessions Court must not await the stage of trial and receive additional evidence to summon another accused, although the powers to add an accused under S. 319 CrPC remain open.

Once the Sessions Court receives the case post committal from the magistrate, it must exercise powers as available to a magistrate, having the complete and unfettered jurisdiction to try the case. The Sessions Court must not act as subservient or powerless deeming it to be a case of the magistrate having already taken cognizance, since it now exercises original jurisdiction in the case. The Sessions Court is, as such, duty bound to find the actual offenders and protect the rights of the parties.

6. Letters of Request

Letters of Request or Letters Rogatory (LR) are a crucial and vital evidence collection mechanism, more specifically in today's time when the cross-border implications of offences are common. These are issued to seek evidence from foreign countries when the police are of the opinion that some vital link or evidence of the case is in a foreign land. Such evidence need not necessarily be documentary in nature but can include the examination of people linked to the case.

Additionally, LRs are an effective mechanism for securing the value of properties situated abroad, both through attachment and seizure, if such property is found to be linked to the commission of offences in the case.

While their importance cannot be denied, a recent pattern, more specifically in white-collar crimes, shows that the investigations and trials are stalled for execution of LRs. Since execution of an LR entails a significant amount of time, it must be ensured that such evidence being sought through the LR is an absolute must for the investigation to be brought to its logical conclusion. Further, to avoid inadvertent delays, the police must strictly follow the Government guidelines for the issuance of LRs.

Mechanism for Issuance of LRs

The guidelines issued by the Government from time to time govern the mode and manner of issuance and execution of LRs. The existing mechanism for issuance of LRs is as under:

1. No request for issuance of LRs be made before any court without the prior concurrence of the Ministry of Home Affairs (MHA).
2. Before making a proposal to the MHA, the officer must examine the necessity to get investigation conducted abroad for taking the case to a logical conclusion.
3. The provisions of the MLAT, MoU, Arrangement or International Convention as well as requirement of the law of the requested country should be studied to ensure that the request falls within the legal parameters of the requested country. The relevant provisions should be duly mentioned in the request.

4. In the absence of any bilateral or multilateral arrangements, LRs may be made based on assurance of reciprocity.
5. Certain countries insist that LRs must be sent in a particular language or format, which must be complied with.
6. For obtaining the concurrence of the MHA, the officer should send the following documents to the MHA:
   a) A self-contained note containing brief facts of the case.
   b) The need to conduct investigation abroad.
   c) The relevant provisions of the MLAT, MoU, etc.
   d) The draft application proposed to be filed in the competent court.
7. Once the MHA approves the request, the application for issuance of LRs be filed before the competent court by the officer.
8. Once the LRs are issued by the court, the officer will forward it to the competent authority in the requested country through defined channels, including the Indian Mission.
9. In event of the requested country seeking clarifications or additional material, the Indian Mission will forward the same to the officer through defined channels, who can then respond to any clarifications/additional material being sought.
10. The execution report, along with evidence and supporting material, received from the requested country would be directly sent by the Indian Mission to the IPCC, CBI, New Delhi, who shall forward it to the police under intimation to the MHA and Ministry of External Affairs.

IV

TRIAL

IV

TRIAL

1. TRIAL STRATEGY

From my experience, it is common for lawyers with multiple engagements to rarely concentrate on one case for days together. As a result, very few lawyers actually strategize their defence at the trial. Also, fewer lawyers strategize at the stage of investigation itself.

For me, trial strategy is a must and should ideally be done during the stage of (1) Pre-investigation, (2) Investigation, (3) Enquiry, and (4) Trial. Let us proceed to deal with these four stages.

Pre-Investigation

Even before the registration of a case, the inkling of a likely investigation can be felt with respect to crimes concerning cheating, forgery, white-collar crimes arising from IPC or special statutes. This, however, may not be the case for violent crimes. One must act on such inkling and intuition and a strategy should be put in place right from that point onwards.

If it comes to it, one must be in a position to explain the allegations with a sensible, viable, and a reasonable narrative of all relevant facts. Else, the investigator who has had a perfunctory look into the papers and has a plan of his own would likely give a narrative of his own. Thereafter, the entire efforts of the defence would be to discredit the said narrative of the investigator and the actual narrative, as such, loses its force.

Investigation

Very few lawyers understand the importance of strategizing during the stage of investigation as the entire concentration during this time is either on (1) avoiding arrest and trying to get anticipatory bail, (2) seeking bail if one is arrested, (3) planning how to dodge delicate questioning or refrain from providing crucial information which may indict the accused, (4) to fire-fight for documents to be given, not to be given and filing applications before the court for such issues where the investigating agency wants to go overboard, therefore necessitating directions to curtail such high-handedness. However, I feel, the concentration should be to strategize in the following manner:

1. If possibility of arrest is high and there are good reasons, only then anticipatory bail should be filed. Else, the effort should be to join investigation and cooperate to the fullest. In doing so, the accused and his defence team can and should focus on the direction of the investigation and in this way, they will be able to read the mind of the investigation agency and pre-empt what they are looking for.
2. In my view, very rarely does the investigating agency completely understand a complex white-collar crime. The investigating agency is at times unable to differentiate between expenses on business exigencies, day-to-day running, salaries, fixed expenses, or even the business losses from the money considered to have been siphoned off by the accused.
3. Thus, this is the time when the entire expense chart under all possible heads should be properly tabulated, documented and submitted to the investigating agency. If such tabulation is accompanied with proper explanations, it will not only help the accused improve his case but will prove to be difficult for the investigation agency to counter it.
4. I may hurry to add that this feature has not properly evolved because either the client is not ready to share such details early on and tries to keep his counsel in the dark or lawyers do not perceive it as important at this stage and feel that there will be further questioning if more details are shared.
5. Speaking for myself, here lies a difference in opinion and it will be naïve for me to say which one is the best course. One thing is for sure, that except in a few cases, the strategy suggested by me is a better way out than not dealing with the facts that will eventually stare at the accused at some stage.

Inquiry

By this time, the charge sheet has been filed and miscellaneous proceedings before the stage of framing of charges are underway. During this time, it is crucial that whatever was given to the investigation agency should be sought for in the form of an application under S. 91 CrPC. If such document or narrative going into the root of the controversy has not been placed on record by the investigating agency or has been distorted, then it must be brought to the notice of the court that the investigation conducted was partisan and unfair.

Trial

After the charge is framed, it is apparent that what the prosecution has to prove needs to be defended. Speaking for myself, I undertake the following exercise at this stage:

1. Preparation of a character sketch of each witness;
2. Critically dissecting the S. 161 statement of the witnesses;
3. Critically examining the documents on which reliance has been placed, if any;
4. Defence lawyers try to conceive what possible improvements the witness can make during his examination-in-chief or if there is an element of surprise that a witness can bring. After discussion of the above, cross-examination questions are made which can be used to discredit the witness and, or the version put by such witness in his cross-examination; and;
5. Special care is taken to bring out such facts which are or should have been in the knowledge of the witness which he has intentionally hidden from the court or has given a coloured version of the same. Such facts are critical for a successful defence cross-examination.

When witnesses of record or witnesses to prove crucial documents are brought, then they should be cross-examined on this basis; (1) the chain of custody not being continuous of safe-keeping and the document could have been tampered; (2) the witness does not possess knowledge of the contents of the document and therefore such document may not be exhibited.

Without elaborating further, it is necessary to give one more example which is of an investigator. The investigator is of prime importance for the defence strategy of the case. All the brainstorming and strategizing in the earlier three stages needs to be brought together to confront the investigator with the material deficiencies that can be pointed out in his investigation as well as the charge sheet. These material exclusions are key to show that the investigation was unfair and thus, the prosecution story put forth also needs to be examined with care and caution.

2. Charge

Amongst some of the important milestones in a criminal trial, the stage of charge has not been given the necessary importance that it deserves. There are also divergent views on the charge expressed at different points in time. On one hand, there is the case of *Yogesh* where discharge was granted in a murder case while agreeing with the settled principle that grave suspicion alone cannot take the place of proof. On the other hand, which is the general practice, charges are framed as a matter of routine, without going into the *prima facie* elements of the crime made out from the charge sheet.

Similarly, there is a wide dichotomy in the approach among the lawyers themselves. There is one school of thought according to which unless there is absolutely no evidence, elaborate arguments at the stage of charge should be avoided while another school of thought feels that effort should be made to highlight the various discrepancies and thus, seek a discharge. Usually, as a construct, a few cases deserve a discharge outright. Therefore, the thought of the first school of not arguing on a charge is based on the premise that while arguing for discharge, the prosecutor would know some of the lacunae or the weaknesses of the case which will be covered up during trial. The other school of thought is primarily based on the rationale for attempting to secure a psychological win to demotivate the PP. Sometimes, such tactics are also implied where clients insist on arguments for discharge or the lawyers try to make a mark and impress clients. Most of the time, such practices boomerang but the rigmarole continues.

Another important issue with respect to framing of charge is that most of the time, the spirit of the offence is not captured, and a faulty charge is usually framed. This is primarily due to the judge not going deeper into the charge sheet, missing out some key elements in the absence of the best assistance required from the PP. Although such charge can be amended at any point of time, many a time, such a mistake leads to complexity in the cases and is detrimental to true justice.

3. Evidence

The prosecution and defence witnesses get their statements recorded on oath. This is where one truly understands the reason why such an individual is brought on the witness list. Both the prosecution and the defence must take a conscious call to not keep an unjustifiably long list of witnesses to protract the trial.

Prosecution Evidence

Examination in Chief

During examination in chief, the prosecutor must bear in mind that the aim of the prosecutor is not to win cases but to assist the court. There may be a situation where a prosecution witness deposes in favour of the accused and it is important for the prosecutor to get that recorded. The defence, on the other hand, should refrain from bringing unnecessary witnesses, who lend no credence to their case and could be demolished in the cross examination.

Sometimes, there may be witnesses who cannot stitch sentences or their answers are not structured, or they might have misinterpreted the question. In all such cases, one must not get flustered or create an environment of animosity for the witness. It would be prudent on the part of the judge to help the witness gather the answers together.

Leading questions are generally not allowed in examination-in-chief or even in re-examination.

Cross-Examination

Cross-examination is perhaps the most challenging as well as the most important facet of a criminal trial. It can single-handedly make or break a case, more specifically since leading questions are permitted to be allowed during cross-examination. For the same reason, it is critical that each word of the deposition of the witness is recorded accurately. The art of cross-examination is discussed in the next chapter.

While each judge writes in his own style, it must be seen that the meaning of the deposition is not changed. Accordingly, audio recording or audio-video recordings of such depositions is done. This will not only prevent inaccurate recording of evidence but will also prevent parties from changing the essence of the answers given by the witnesses. This practice is in stark contrast to the West where no one can change the statements made and all comments are also made a part of the record. The judges there have absolutely no authority to add or delete a word.

Re-examination

Re-examination is not to be permitted to fill a lacuna in the case. It is generally used only for the purposes of clarification and without any change in the version already put forward by the witness. Though it is a power to be allowed by the judge sparingly, the prevalent practice of almost barring any re-examination should not be followed. This becomes all the more critical in cases of rustic witnesses who do not understand the intricacies of the question asked. Neither the prosecution nor the defence should be allowed to take advantage of such a situation.

Statement of Accused under Section 313 CrPC

Another facet of our criminal justice system is the examination of the accused in line with the principles of natural justice. This stage arises once the prosecution evidence is closed. The courts are duty bound to record such statements under S. 313 CrPC, put each incriminating material to the accused, and seek his explanation in this regard. All such circumstances not put to the accused cannot be used against him and are excluded from consideration. In a case of circumstantial evidence, such statements are essential to decide whether or not the chain of circumstances is complete.

While such statements are not recorded on oath and cannot form the sole basis of conviction since they are not a substantive piece of evidence, they can nonetheless be used for appreciating the prosecution evidence. The said parameters however take a back seat should the accused himself choose to depose as a defence witness under S. 315 CrPC.

It is at the closing stage of a S. 313 CrPC statement that the accused is asked by the court if he wants to lead evidence. Depending on the circumstances of the case, if the accused chooses to lead evidence, then the case will proceed to the stage of defence evidence. Such a stage would not arise if the accused chooses to not lead any defence evidence, more so if the defence feels that the prosecution has failed to establish any case. In such circumstances, the case will directly proceed to the stage of final arguments.

Defence Evidence

In case the accused chooses to lead defence evidence, he is required to inform the court of the witnesses he proposes to examine. If required, the accused may request the court to summon such witnesses. Usually, formal witnesses are summoned by the court. The mode and manner of leading of defence evidence is the same as prosecution evidence, which has already been discussed above.

The Supreme Court, in a celebrated case, has stated that defence evidence is to be treated at par with prosecution evidence but in day-to-day working of the court one realizes that the defence evidence does not get the same probative value as is given to the prosecution evidence.

Recording of Evidence during Trial: Way Forward

A criminal trial is a lengthy process and each trial lasts longer than the other. At present, solutions for this issue are being actively looked at by the courts and many such processes are put in place to expedite trials. Each stakeholder in the trial shoulders the responsibility to ensure timely disposal of cases. In this regard, my suggestions are as follows:

1. There is a need to devise a system where trials are time bound.
2. No adjournments should be granted by courts for frivolous reasons. The court must strictly restrict to granting a maximum of one adjournment per side throughout the trial. If further adjournments are necessary, it is for litigants and lawyers to make alternative arrangements.
3. A period of 10 days, as mutually decided by parties and as per the convenience of court, must be fixed by the courts at the outset for the evidence.
4. Formal witnesses must be bound down and cross-examined in one day.

5. The complainant and victims should be willing to get their evidence recorded on any given day and time.
6. There is a need to implement a day-to-day trial scheme, as is the intent under the CrPC.
7. Courts must be critical of long cross-examinations and repetitions. If the cross-examination is also being done to delay the trial or the party is seeking accommodation to cross-examine the witness without any justifiable cause, the cross-examination should be closed. The conduct of lawyers and witnesses should also be noted for reference by the judge.
8. Young lawyers must not be given adjournments for the non-availability of seniors and should be encouraged to proceed with the case.
9. The courts must ensure that equal weightage is given to the defence and prosecution witnesses.
10. The investigator is also a crucial witness and the lapses in discharge of duties, which may be highlighted during his examination, must also be given great weightage in arriving at a conclusion regarding his impartiality.
11. The expeditious disposal of a trial requires competency and skill by lawyers. A trial is truly an art, and its flair is possessed by only a few. The members of the legal fraternity must remember to train young lawyers and not patronize those attempting to learn this skill.
12. The judge must also make notes and record his observations about the demeanour of the witness. This would have a direct bearing on the credibility of the witness. It would not only help in the future adjudication of the case but also help another judge decide the case in situations where the matter is transferred or even the same judge to refresh his memory.

Trial in Absentia and Segregation of Trial

Apart from the aforesaid, a common problem faced by the courts in expeditious recording of evidence is the difficulty in securing the presence of the accused. Section 299 of the CrPC envisages such a challenge and provides for the concept of recording of evidence in the absence of the accused who has either absconded, refused from appearing before court or there is no immediate prospect of him returning from abroad to face trial. In such a scenario, the trial of the absconding accused is segregated and can be revisited once such accused is present or brought before court. This provision helps save the time of the court and prevent prolonged delay in trial, thereby facilitating the right to a speedy trial.

4. Art of Cross-Examination

Cross-examination is more dangerous than a trapeze artist performing, who is always a step away from a devastating fall. The knowledge of law alone is not a solution to conduct an effective cross-examination, one must also possess as well as develop the skill to become a good cross-examiner.

Cross-examination in some way is something that we have been doing in our daily lives when we interact with individuals socially, professionally or even personally. However, unlike these situations where we might get another chance, cross-examination in a criminal trial has no second chances. One good or bad question while conducting the cross-examination has the potential to change the outcome of a criminal trial.

The witness narrates his version of the case under oath during his examination-in-chief. During cross-examination, questions can be put to the witness based on the evidence of the witness recorded or his statements recorded under S.161 CrPC. Limits of cross-examination are not strictly confined to examination-in-chief and there is freedom to ask any question which can impeach the credibility of the witness or doubt the version put forward by him within the confines of the Evidence Act.

However, one cannot always be sure of the answers given by the witness during his cross-examination. That is why the power and impact of each question, and its timing cannot be underestimated. One question may either discredit the witness, uncover the fallacies in his version or jeopardize a good case. The ability to identify and ask the right questions is derived from an understanding of law, logic and the intuition of a lawyer.

Objective of Cross-Examination

In criminal law, the stakes are high. There are always three sides to the story—the one told by the complainant, the other by the police and the third by the defence. The defence is not concerned with the truth but has to put forth its theory to discredit the complainant or the investigation, or create a doubt with regard to the authenticity of the prosecution case. Basically, in a criminal trial, the onus on the prosecution is to prove their case beyond reasonable doubt whereas the onus on the defence is to bring out an element of doubt in the story of the prosecution.

The objectives of cross-examination are (i) discovery of truth in a given case; (ii) espousing falsehood in the case or the stand taken; (iii) discredit the testimony of the witness; and (iv) bring out the undisclosed side of the case. The undisclosed side of the case is critical when the prosecution may not have reached the entire truth and is used by the defence to demolish the case. While on the ground, prosecutor is limited to a script and can only make minor changes, there is nothing to stop the defence from asking any questions in cross-examination, provided that they must be relevant and admissible.

There are times when the defence commits an error in getting some witnesses to strengthen its case but the prosecutor gets a chance to bring out what the investigator and the prosecution as a whole failed to prove in their prosecution evidence. A good cross-examination by the prosecution in such cases helps the prosecutor to strengthen his case. The 1984 riots case was one example which comes to my mind where the conviction was secured largely by the cross-examination of defence witnesses.

Importance of the Evidence Act during Cross-examination—'RAW is WAR'

The Evidence Act is the key for understanding the procedure of cross-examination, which governs not only criminal trials but also civil trials and arbitrations. As told by Paul Pfau, a teacher in California, the understanding of the Evidence Act can be conceptualised by using the WWE mantra, 'RAW IS WAR', where 'R' stands for Relevancy; 'A' stands for Admissibility; and 'W' stands for Witness.

'R'—Relevancy

No question can be asked during cross-examination if it is not relevant. An important prerequisite of a cross-examination is that the question must have a certain degree of relevance attached to it. The judge will many a time stop and ask why is the question relevant? If one cannot satisfy the judge on this point, such question would be disallowed. Similarly, there may be times that the opposition raises an objection on the relevancy of a question, which will then be decided by the judge.

'A'—Admissibility

Depending on the surrounding circumstances, the admissibility of a fact or document gains importance. Admissibility of the fact or document depends on its relevancy and its foundation. While laying the foundation, a lawyer must introduce the fact or document to the witness by putting a question pertaining to the witness's knowledge of the said fact or document or related details. If a witness denies having any knowledge of the document or question, the admissibility of the question or document vanishes. The lawyer cannot proceed further unless he can show that such witness is deposing falsely. If the witness again answers and denies having any knowledge, then the lawyer must either drop further questions on the issue or possess clinching evidence to contradict the witness.

'W'—Witness

Understanding a witness, his type and his role involves keeping in mind the legal principles as well as the fact in issue. In order to strategize and know what one wants from a witness, the objective of examining him and the questions to be put to him, one must know what type of witness he or she is.

It is a high-pressure situation for both the lawyer as well as the witness, who is under oath to state the truth. Thus, not only is there any moral pressure but also a legal pressure on the witness to answer truthfully. This fear and pressure is often used by lawyers to their advantage while cross-examining the witness, either directly or indirectly. Though this is a good tactic, it must not lead to unnecessary harassment of the witness. The witness must only be reminded of the need to answer truthfully and not misuse the law.

Once the understanding of 'RAW is WAR' is thorough, half the battle of conducting a fruitful cross-examination is won.

A few pointers to keep in mind during Cross-examination

1. The job of the prosecutors is not to oversee the success of the case but to assist the court. He must have the courage to tell the judge if a witness has been won over or is deposing falsely. Most prosecutors in India are fair and do not cross the line to become persecutors. They, like any lawyer, are fighting their case but they draw a line at making sure that their actions are fair. Such conduct of prosecutors in our system is commendable. One must remember that being fair yields better results.
2. For the defence, they bring witnesses to discredit the prosecution case. A defence counsel must remember that in case he is of the opinion that the prosecution case has been sufficiently discredited, he must refrain from bringing further witnesses since questions asked during cross-examination can turn the tables.
3. Each defence lawyer must attempt to use his cross-examining skills to get the witness to come out with such answers that he had intended to seek to dent the prosecution story and/or discredit the witness.
4. Prior to the cross-examination, lawyers should know which witnesses they wish to cross-examine who have a material bearing on the case. Lawyers should also have a broad idea of what they wish to achieve and uncover during cross-examination.
5. Lawyers from either side should not go overboard in asking too many questions, despite strong temptations. They must carefully assess whether the risk is worth taking or not. Even while taking a risk, the lawyer must try to put those questions which have only one answer. For any other answer, the lawyer must have sufficient proof to confront the witness.
6. An important aspect of cross-examination is suggestions. If a lawyer has a theory and is not able to bring out the same through his questioning, he may put suggestions based on his theory to the witness. These suggestions must however find support by other evidence testimonies or from the circumstances of the case.

7. One must always remember that learning the art of cross-examination is a continuing process and only practice and experience can develop the requisite skills.

Observations made by a judge during Cross-examination

While recording testimonies of witnesses, the judge notices and forms his opinion on the credibility of the witness and his demeanour or anything which the judge feels is significant to be a part of the record. This later helps the judge analyse which evidence is to be relied upon for making his final decision. However, judges are often transferred during the pendency of a case and the new judge is not privy to the demeanour or credibility of the witnesses examined. Thus, it is crucial for all judges to pen down their observations for their future reference as well as for the benefit of the succeeding judges in case of transfer. In this way, even the appellate court would be able to grasp the nuances of the testimony of the witness or pay weightage to his demeanour.

To sum up, the practice of judges recording their remarks during witness examination must be adopted and encouraged. These observations, made in real time, can be utilized to analyse the testimony of witnesses in its true spirit.

5. Summoning of Additional Accused

During the course of the proceedings, the court may find that there is evidence against a person regarding the commission of the offence and such person has not been charge-sheeted. In such a scenario, S. 319 CrPC enables the court to initiate proceedings against such persons to do complete justice and ensure that persons who ought to have been tried are also tried. Such a provision enables the court in the administration of justice and prevent the real perpetrators of crime from going unpunished.

Such powers can be exercised during inquiry and trial. While inquiry commences post the filing of charge sheet, trial is said to commence once the charge is framed. As such, the power under S. 319 CrPC can be exercised by the court at any time post filing of the charge sheet till the pronouncement of judgment, except during the stage of compliances for supply of documents to the accused and committal to the Court of Sessions, which are administrative steps and do not require a judicial application of mind.

At the stage of inquiry, invoking S. 319 CrPC is restricted to only such persons added in column 2 of the charge sheet or any other person who might be an accomplice, since the court only has the charge sheet for a *prima facie* case to find out as to whether a person, who can be an accused, has been erroneously omitted or deliberately excluded by the prosecuting agencies. Any other material collected during inquiry by the court is to corroborate the evidence recorded during trial. During trial, there is no such restriction on the exercise of power since the court is seized of the evidence in the case. Such a power can be as such exercised at any stage during the trial and the court need not even wait for a witness to be cross-examined.

S. 319 CrPC however is an extra ordinary power and must be exercised only when the court has strong and cogent evidence. The degree of satisfaction must be more from the stage of charge but short of the satisfaction of conviction.

6. Arguments

For a lawyer, after the hard work of the prosecution and the defence, arguments are just the final stage to make an impact to win a desired verdict. Very few lawyers prepare a holistic argument which is incisive, precise and, or cutting edge. Many a time, lawyers refer to the portion of the testimonies of the witnesses that suits them and base their arguments on them. Such arguments are buttressed with favourable judgments. Incidentally, both sides use such formulas in almost every case. However, to my mind, the success of a good argument lies in satisfying the following:

For the Prosecution

1. The proof of the ingredients of the offence alleged.
2. The testimony of the victim and the relevant witnesses proving the offences.
3. Highlighting an impartial investigation when put under doubt by the defence.
4. The impact on the victims and/or society at large.

For the Defence

1. Creating a doubt in the narrative of the prosecution.
2. Highlighting that the ingredients of the offence alleged are not met with.
3. Demonstrating discrepancies in the statement of witnesses and the evidence.
4. Highlighting what has not been brought by the prosecution including not examining the necessary witnesses or not placing on record crucial documents, or anything that would have cleared the name of the accused.
5. Pointing out the deficiencies in the investigation, especially the absence of scientific evidence or potential natural witnesses.

There are some cases which by their very nature are brutal and which shock the conscience of society at large. The judge has an onus to ensure that such cases, which entail a strict or higher punishment, also satisfy a higher degree of proof while the defence in such circumstances should try to create more than the regular doubt to seek benefit.

In today's context, it is advisable especially for the defence to give the written summary of the arguments to ensure that a judge deals with all the arguments. Also, it becomes important in the appeal to show to the appellate court that the judgment does or does not reflect all the arguments raised by the defence and to show that some critical points have not been dealt with by the judge. The Appellate Court should take notice of such conduct of the trial judge.

However, one must not lose sight of the fact that a judge is human and also a member of society. Like any other person, many a time, a judge has his own biases and prejudices as part of his persona. A good lawyer should have, amongst other things, a deeper understanding of the persona of the judge during the trial and more so during arguments. To conclude, the lawyer from either side should be able to place correct facts, the position of law in brief and the requisites of burden of proof to be highlighted in unambiguous terms. The totality of these factors is impactful and touches the judicial conscience of the judges.

7. Judgment

Pre-Requisites

S. 353 and S. 354 CrPC deal with the pronouncement of judgment. Besides the technicality of pronouncement and the language in which it is to be pronounced, the CrPC spells out the following essentials to be contained in the judgment based on its content:

1. Points for determination, decision thereon and the reason for the decision.
2. Relief granted or sentence awarded; and
3. Reasoning vis-à-vis facts and law.

Most judgments spell out the factual matrix, the summary of witness accounts, the summary of the arguments from both sides and reason it on the basis of judgments, if at all relied upon by the counsels while addressing the arguments. However, largely, it has been seen that the judge already makes up his mind to acquit and convict the accused persons during the trial and after hearing the arguments. Thus, judgments at times solely comprise of the evidence and arguments which favour a particular verdict of acquittal or conviction. Therefore, in addition to what is provided under S. 354 CrPC, the judge, in his judgments, should mention or deal with the following:

1. All issues raised by the prosecution and defence without being selective.
2. After dealing with the factual matrix and the arguments addressed, an issue-wise discussion so that no issue raised by either side goes unanswered.
3. While the judgments usually have a critical analysis of the witnesses, they will be further enhanced if the judge gives a brief account of the demeanour of the witnesses.

Proposal

It is proposed that after having heard the arguments and having gone through the evidence, besides noting the above, it is essential that a judge also does the following:

1. Foremost, every judgment should point out the conduct of the investigator who has charge-sheeted the accused with respect to.:
    a. Impartiality of investigation.
    b. Quality of the investigation
    c. Competence in the collection of evidence
    d. All the relevant disclosures having been factored in, which otherwise he found or could have found favouring the accused.
2. With respect to the complainant, wherever the judge finds false involvement or over implication of accused persons or the allegations being exaggerated, the judge should mention those facts and proceed to charge the complainant for false implication. These should be summary proceedings, where the complainant should be given a chance to defend his claims.

The said proposal would help achieve the following results:

1. Reduce false cases being registered.
2. The complainant and investigator being more responsible and impartial.
3. Help in the better delivery of justice.
4. Restoration of public faith; and
5. Less load on the judicial system which is otherwise overburdened.

Most courts in their hearts are usually not convinced with the investigation or prosecution. They are thus hesitant in imposing adequate compensation for the victim. In an ideal system based on the proposal given above, the conviction of the judge will be much more to liberally exercise powers and award compensation to the victim.

8. Consequences and Considerations of Sentencing

Post-conviction sentencing, in case the judgment results in the conviction of an accused, triggers a host of provisions under CrPC. Some of them include Ss. 357, 357-A, 360, 361 CrPC amongst others. These sections are of great importance. However, the sad reality is that they are rarely adverted to in their true spirit.

Compensation for Victims

The courts rarely award compensation in favour of victims. Either there is no compensation at all or in rare circumstances if compensation is granted, it is inadequate. Generally, the fine imposed while sentencing an accused is not made a part of victim compensation. This fine is usually in terms of punishable sections where sentence is rigorous imprisonment and not in terms of S. 357 CrPC.

Probation for Accused

In favour of the accused, there are statutory provisions of S. 360 and 361 CrPC. The release of an accused on probation in all cases where sentence is up to seven years is envisaged under S. 360. It is often invoked when the offender has been convicted for the first time. S. 360 CrPC also envisages a category wherein a person less than 21 years of age or a woman who has been accorded a sentence less that life imprisonment and who is a first-time offender is accorded probation on good conduct. Further, S. 361 envisages that if the court is not inclined to release the person on probation, irrespective of whether he is to be convicted for the first time, there must be special reasons provided in writing. However, in the present scheme of the criminal justice system, neither S. 360 nor S. 361 of CrPC have been given the due consideration that they demand. It is strange that in my 33 years of practice, neither I have read nor have I experienced the use of S. 360 CrPC in cases where the punishment is more than seven years.

Besides the CrPC, the emphasis on probation has been the intent of the legislature which is evident from the fact that a separate enactment was made, namely, Probation of Offenders Act, 1958. However, it is unfortunate that even with such an Act in existence, its provisions have rarely been adverted to. The judiciary is also responsible for not promoting the probation of offenders on good conduct except for some rare judgments. Such judgments at the same time have, however, failed to consider the intent of the legislature in its true perspective.

Pardon and Remission

Another post-trial benefit to the accused is by way of pardons, respite, reprieves, remissions, or to suspend, remit, or commute the sentence, which power rests with the executive. Courts have rightly derived a mechanism for judicial review of such exercise of executive powers. In practicality, the executive exercises these powers in a manner that the same is applicable across broad parameters. Very rarely do we see invocation of these powers in individual cases or for marginal sections of society. The only time such power is exercised by the executive is usually for an influential person. This leads to a hue and cry both in the media and public and the salutary provision is thereby given a restrictive meaning by the courts.

Recommendations

Overall, few recommendations in brief which must be weighed by the courts while sentencing a convict are as follows:

1. At the time of sentencing, the judge must only hear the state and the accused and not the victim, since the victim has already played his part in securing conviction of the accused. It is only when the victim argues for a balancing act should the judge hear him for the purposes of sentencing.
2. There is a need to assess the surrounding circumstances as to why the convict committed the offence, that is, in the heat of the moment, mental conditions, and the like. These factors may not affect his guilt but affect the sentencing, more specifically in offences with life sentence. It is important to prioritize saving individuals from jail especially since when sentencing is for reformation.
3. There is a need to revise the process of reformation since the scheme is very mechanical, technical, and tedious. If parole facilitates the accused to connect with society and family, the impact of parole

on the psyche and mind of the convict must be analysed once he returns from parole. Such analysis weighs in while assessing the suspension of sentence of the accused.

4. A liberal approach must be adopted for first-time offenders.
5. In cases of acquittal, the judge must also apply S. 357-A CrPC for compensating the accused falsely implicated, since such accused is also a victim who has been subjected to the rigours of trial and has faced adversity.
6. S. 360 and S. 361 CrPC, which deal with probation for good conduct, should be kept in mind for compensation. In appropriate cases, the court should devise strict punishment without remissions, which will serve as a deterrent.
7. Lastly, the court should not be swayed by public sentiments or media pressure but should be guided by the principles of law.

V

POST-TRIAL CONSIDERATIONS

Introduction

The trial results in either conviction or acquittal. In case of a conviction, the accused has a right to file an appeal whereas in case of an acquittal, the State, if it chooses to challenge the acquittal, can file an appeal under S. 378 CrPC. In 2009, there was an amendment to S. 372 CrPC through which, in cases of acquittal, even the victim has a right to prefer an appeal. This right of the victim has been made absolute and there exists no requirement to seek any leave to prefer this appeal.

Ways to Deal with an Appeal

Filing of an appeal in criminal cases has undergone a huge change. Traditionally, a few decades ago, old school lawyers used to simply file an appeal practically with only one ground, that is, *"That the judgment does not merit to stand on the factual matrix and on the appreciation of law"*. It was done simply because the appeal being an extension of the trial would lead the appellate court to appreciate the entire evidence on record and not simply critically evaluate the judgment passed by the trial court. In effect, the judges, except for considering the suspension of sentence, would not look into the judgment passed by the trial court and would arrive at their own findings based on the evaluation of the evidence on record. On the contrary, today, although the courts agree with the principle, the findings recorded by the trial courts do sway them and the lawyers also freely refer to the judgment passed by the trial court in appeal. Elaborate appeals with grounds and reasoning are filed, since these are expected to be filed, even by courts.

It is not really the issue as to which approach is right or wrong. The old school reasoning seems to be that the appellate court should independently evaluate the evidence on record simply because it should arrive at the conclusion based on the evidence and the arguments raised before it. Even elaborate grounds in drafting an appeal are not needed since the evidence itself has to be read again.

There is a vast difference of opinion in practice even before the Supreme Court. Two decades ago, even though Special Leave Petitions used to be dismissed as they are today, the parties were given an elaborate hearing once leave was granted and the matter was converted into an appeal. As such, a full hearing used to be given while deciding the appeal. It was the endeavour of the court that justice is done to an extent that the lawyer feels that he has been heard and the end result is after giving a fair hearing to the parties. However, today, either because of the pendency of cases or the changed surroundings, the criminal appeals are seemingly more and more summarily decided. Judges are swayed by the findings of the courts below and many a time, a reading of the judgments by the lower courts is sufficient to dispose of the appeal.

I cannot but mention a strange practice that has evolved in the High Courts and the Supreme Court while hearing appeals. A judge is very often seen asking the lawyer the following questions:

1. Why have you not asked this question to a witness?
2. Why did you not clarify while examining the witness which could have proved a particular instance?
3. Why did you not cross-examine a particular witness?
4. Why did you not produce some defence evidence?

Such a list of questions goes on. Such questions are utterly strange since the onus of proving the case beyond reasonable doubt is upon the prosecution and has to be discharged by it. As is commonly put, the prosecution has to stand on its own feet.

It is a matter of common prudence that if something has not been brought in evidence, no defence lawyer worth his salt will ask a question which has the potential of being answered in a manner that could compromise the defence of the accused. Also, since the onus is only to create a doubt, it is not the duty of the defence to disprove a fact beyond reasonable doubt. This practice which has evolved has been responsible for dismissing a large number of cases which is against the spirit of the criminal justice system that has been in existence for a long time. Such unwanted departures made by the judiciary have come in the way of dispensing justice. In my very humble view, the reason that I see in such departure is because most judges have not conducted defence trials. Therefore, they do not appreciate the difficulties faced by defence lawyers who have an onerous task of defending an accused against whom a natural bias on its face exists.

Suspension of Sentence (Bail)

Bail would depend upon the period undergone or the punishment that has been granted to the accused. While up to three years, the trial court itself grants bail which is generally confirmed by the appellate court, bails in cases of punishment up to seven years are usually granted if the courts deem it fit, depending on various considerations, including the following:

1. Factual matrix of case;
2. Period undergone during trial;
3. Gravity of the offence;
4. If the person has been on bail and has not misused the liberty granted to him.

However, in cases of sentences of 10 years or more, bail is more difficult in an appeal in cases of conviction. Such bail is usually renewed after the person has spent a considerable time in jail and his appeal is not likely to be heard in the near future.

Additional Evidence and Other Proceedings at Appellate Stage such as Parole and Premature Release

One of the rarest exercised powers during appeal is adducing additional evidence under S. 391 CrPC. Though worded widely, the onus and rigours attached to these powers make it difficult for the court to exercise these powers as no party to the proceeding is generally allowed to fill the gaps during appeal. The fundamental test to determine whether additional evidence must be adduced is the satisfaction of the appellate court about the necessity of such evidence for deciding the appeal. This necessity may not be for the impossibility to pronounce the judgment but for any failure of justice without it.

Some of the other important litigations that one can see in the courts relate to the exercise of powers of parole and premature releases, based on remissions or good conduct, or in terms of rules as per jail manual and such other reasons. While this law laid down by the Supreme Court in the case of *Maru Ram* holds good, there have been many aberrations on premature releases under the CrPC, which are as such different from the premature releases approved by the Governor or President. Even in cases involving life sentence, the courts have dealt with the issue differently. Although the Supreme Court has said that life means life but, by law, it was made 14 years after which premature release could be considered. However, over a period of time, depending upon the gravity, courts have started writing the meaning of life. Regardless, the same would not stop the Governor or the President from exercising the powers granted to them while granting release to the convict.

VI

THE BIG PICTURE

Although there is a certain kind of conclusion for every topic dealt in this book, there are some fundamental issues that I feel need reiteration. The Republic of India is growing in stature in the world community—be it politically, economically or socially—and it will get a place of pride when the country can demonstrate to the world that the rule of law exists, irrespective of any claim. At present, however, the rule of law is diminishing in the arena of criminal justice.

This book gives a pragmatic and logical understanding of the existing legal framework. While dissecting the criminal justice system, it brings forth the realities of how law is used by and for each stakeholder today. Such reality is indicative of an emerging need to evolve law and its procedure with the changing needs of society.

In this book, important aspects of criminal procedure have been examined in a manner where issues faced or those bound to crop up have been identified, along with proposed solutions to overcome them. These solutions address a peculiar problem in the scheme of ensuring that the rule of law and, invariably, justice prevails. That is, by and large, the emphasis of this book.

However, if one needs to suggest 10 most important measures to ensure overall health and viability of the criminal justice system, the same are as under:

1. Meaningful and proper access to justice for the common man, both in terms of affordability and reach.
2. Timebound and impartial investigations.
3. Accountability of the investigating officers in cases of *mala fide* use of power.
4. Strict action against false implication and over-implication of accused.
5. Arrest should be the last resort and the necessity of arrest must be shown in writing. Bail jurisprudence needs to be revisited. Liberal in bail and stricter in sentencing should be the way forward.
6. Pre-trial processes have to be quick and simplified.
7. Timebound conclusion of trials. Extensions can be allowed only by higher courts in exceptional cases.

8. The autonomy of the lower judiciary needs to be protected from the administrative control of their respective High Courts. Lower courts should be encouraged to fearlessly exercise their minds and explore law to address unique issues.
9. Need for appointment of judges in the Supreme Court who have experience in conducting trials.
10. Investigators, lawyers and judges must practise self-discipline and maintain high moral and ethical standards.

If we adhere to these, it will not only help in saving national resources but will also promote the rule of law in India.

INDEX

CASES